There aren't all that many books widely available on the art of storyboarding (when compared to other creative fields), much less one I've read with such a simple overview on the world of freelancing. Covering (as the title suggests) the worlds of advertising, film, and TV, this is a comprehensive guide to those starting out in the field. I'd also consider this worth a read for those looking to hire storyboard artists—it's always good to know exactly what is reasonable to request of creative professionals.

—Erin Corrado. www.onemoviefiveviews.com

Terrific! The under-appreciated dark art of storyboarding is illuminated here. Everything about the art and business of a storyboard artist is brilliantly framed.

—John Badham, director, creator of ShotMaster
jbbadhamcompany.com

A practical guide that is, like its subject, a conceptual and physical tool for saving time and money. Recommended for film students looking for illumination of all corners of the filmmaking process (and possibly to discover a niche) and freelance artists seeking a change.

—Ben Malczewski, *Library Journal*

With this book, Peppe does for storyboard artists what Scott McCloud's Understanding Comics did for comics. Crisp, highly informative, and essential in understanding the language of the medium. Great stuff!

—Greg Ruth, comic artist, *The Matrix, Conan, Creepy, Freaks of the Heartland*

The Storyboard Artist gives a well-designed and comprehensive overview for anyone setting out on a career in the field. It will benefit professionals as well because of its fresh perspective on the tools of the trade. Giuseppe's fine drawings show a passion for the storytelling medium. This book will have a permanent place on my shelf.

—Trevor Goring, illustrator/storyboard artist/graphic novelist, *Independence Day, Mission Impossible II, Twilight*

It is my pleasure, both to have had Giuseppe Cristiano work for me, creating terrific storyboards for the Nickelodeon animated series 3 Friends and Jerry, and now to recommend this new book. Succeeding as a professional storyboard artist is not easy. It requires not only excellent storytelling and decent drawing skills but many others as well, all-too-often overlooked in art school: marketing, task management, and navigating the chaos of the get-it-done-yesterday world of film and TV production. This book offers the aspiring storyboard artist an education in all of these. Read and keep The Storyboard Artist next to your desk. You will not only have the tools to become a better storyboarder: you will have the benefit of a seasoned professional mentor at your side.

—Ray Kosarin, producer/director, *Daria, Beavis and Butt-Head, Da Mob, The World of Tosh*; animation instructor, New York University's Tisch School of the Arts

At last! A great book on the most important step in filmmaking—the storyboards.

—Bill Plympton, animator/director/screenwriter/ producer, *Plymptoons, The Tune, I Married a Strange Person!, Mutant Aliens, Hair High,* and *Idiots*

GIUSEPPE CRISTIANO **THE**

STORYBOARD

A GUIDE TO FREELANCING IN FILM, TV, AND ADVERTISING **ARTIST**

WITHDRAWN

Published by Michael Wiese Productions
12400 Ventura Blvd., # 1111
Studio City, CA 91604
tel. 818.379.8799
fax 818.986.3408
mw@mwp.com
www.mwp.com

Cover Art: Giuseppe Cristiano
Book Design: Gina Mansfield Design
Editor: Pamela Grieman

All photos, illustrations, and storyboards
by Giuseppe Cristiano, except:
Ulrika Sjöberg: Photos on page 11 and 15
Marco Letizia: Comics on page 21, 60; and illustrations on
pages 29, 138 (illustrations 2, 3), 154
Alessandra Orlacchio: illustration 1 on page 34
Massimigliano Pugliese: Photos on Pages 106, 107, 108, 109
Tomas Skoging: Storyboard Sketches on page 103
Jean "Moebius" Giraud: Illustration on page 178

Special Thanks:
My Family, Per Carlsson, Fredrik Norberg,
Frederic Pascual (for the cover illustration),
Cynthia Prescher, and Daniel Arvor.

Printed by McNaughton & Gunn, Inc., Saline, Michigan
Manufactured in the United States of America
Printed on Recycled Stock

Library of Congress Cataloging-in-Publication Data

Cristiano, Giuseppe.
The storyboard artist : a guide to freelancing in film, TV, and advertising /
Giuseppe Cristiano.
    p. cm.
Includes bibliographical references.
ISBN 978-1-61593-083-8
1. Storyboards. 2. Commercial art--Technique. 3. Motion pictures--Production
and direction. I. Title.
NC1002.S85C74 2012
741.6023--dc23
                                        2011038438

DEDICATION

To Clara and Lorenzo, my mum and dad.

For the inspiration and the motivation that led me into professional storyboarding I'd like to mention Mr. Jean Giraud, aka Moebius, whom I had the fortune to meet in real life a few times, and who was kind enough to invite me to his studio. I received from him cherished advice, as well as some fabulous books I proudly keep in my collection.

I would also like to thank all of the directors with whom I had the pleasure to work and from whom I learned a great deal of information, techniques, and tricks of the trade. Thank you for the experiences that made me grow. Among the many are Jonas Åkerlund, Fredrik Bond, Johan Kamitz, Eric Broms, Sam Brown, Johan Renck, Tomas Skoging, and many more.

A very special thank you goes to Ray Kosarin, director of *Beavis and Butt-head*, *Daria*, *3 Friends & Jerry*, and the *Saturday Night Live* cartoons, who taught me the patience and fun of working with animation.

Thanks also go to the advertising agencies all around the world that I work with regularly: Saatchi & Saatchi, DDB, McCann Worldgroup, Ogilvy, Leo Burnett, BBDO Worldwide, and many more.

And, of course, the film and TV production companies I worked with throughout the years deserve special thanks, including Universal, Warner Bros., Fox Family, HBO, BBC, RAI, Ridley Scott Associates, Aardman Animations, Nelvana, SF (Svensk Filmindustri), Nordisk Film, Stink, Rogue, and the list goes on.

Last, but not least, I want to thank all of the people I had the pleasure to draw on my boards: Paul Newman, Clint Eastwood, Robert DeNiro, Gene Simmons of Kiss, Lemmy from Motörhead, Steven Seagal, Madonna, and others.

ACKNOWLEDGMENTS

CONTENTS

INTRODUCTION

A good artist catches the frame, but a good frame catches the artist.

My intention with this book wasn't just to write yet another storyboard manual. It was my goal to produce a book that covers all aspects of the storyboard profession and that focuses, to a large extent, on the creativity required by an artist in order to accomplish the work in the best possible way. My goal is to provide useful information for those who are interested in exploring or pursuing a storyboarding career.

As a professional, I understand that a good storyboard artist is not simply someone who is a great artist. There is much more involved. A storyboard freelancer is one who is capable of resolving problems and finding solutions while working on a script with other creative types such as art directors, copywriters, and movie directors. The storyboard profession entails much more than just possessing the ability to draw; therefore, this book will cover many other aspects of the storyboard profession.

Start at the beginning of the manual and take notes as you read through it. By the time you finish the manual, you will have acquired all of the basics needed to launch your freelance storyboard career. I wish you all the best!

Sincerely,
Giuseppe Cristiano

How to Use This Book

When I started writing this book, I had in mind to address not just the artist per se, but all of the people involved in production who would deal with the storyboard in one way or another. It occurred to me that sometimes the ones who hire me for storyboarding do not understand or remember the purpose or meaning of the board, and I have to explain it to them or remind them of it. So this prompted me to write a book that would be educational and provide instruction for all members of the production team.

As an example, it's not very often that I work with cinematographers, but when I do, the camera work would benefit from a well-planned storyboard. It's always useful to know the why and how of certain techniques. With this book, it's my intention to teach not only technique, but also the application of it for a job well done.

I have included some personal stories, as well as some advice and tips from my own bag of tricks that I hope will inspire young talents. I advise the hungry artist to work through the exercises I provide in this book. I hope they will help you as much as they helped me.

I would like this book to be a guide, not only for the artist, but also for the professionals in need of a good storyboard artist. The guide will help them know what questions to ask when selecting an artist for a specific job, and help them understand what to expect from the job. I have included original artwork and samples from my archives to give an idea of what actual jobs might look like.

In the guide, I talk a lot about organization. I can't stress it enough: Organization is a must in the storyboard profession. I hope my personal tips on organization are useful for you. You will learn some tips of your own as you go, but applying the ones I have listed in the guide will get you started and keep you on track.

I wish you the best of luck and much success.

STORYBOARD DETAILS

What Is a Storyboard?

Storyboards are commonly referred to as a series of illustrations or frames used to visualize scenes of a script that directors and film crews work from during the shooting of a movie. Sometimes people make the mistake of referring to the storyboard as the comic strip version of the script. However, this is not an accurate reference, as the work of a storyboard artist and the work of a comic strip artist are a world apart and require a completely different approach in the planning, execution, and finalization of the work. The only thing the storyboard artist and the comic strip have in common is that both are skilled artists who work with pen and paper.

The storyboard is the backbone of a production, a tool that helps a director visualize the work he or she is going to produce. The storyboard provides the director with the opportunity to fine-tune a script before the shooting starts. This is advantageous to any director for preventing mistakes and wasted time.

The storyboard can also be used as a budgeting tool. The production company can study the storyboard and determine all the costs and necessities of the film, as well as plan for the amount of time needed for shooting. The storyboard will let the production company know how to choose location, cast, and special effects, as well as organize the shooting work. The producer can also use the storyboard as a tool for acquiring funding for a film.

Storyboarding is widely present in the advertising industry and vital for the animation in the video game industry. And yet, this widespread profession is rarely heard about. Even in film schools or colleges, storyboarding is rarely talked about, except in passing. There are very few books on the subject.

When I started my storyboarding career, I had no idea what I was getting into. To be honest, storyboarding didn't seem like a very fine or interesting profession to me. It didn't excite me as much as the idea of drawing comics, which is what I was doing when I stumbled into storyboarding by chance. I was contacted as a last resort by an advertising agency that was desperate to find someone to produce something for a very specific medium: television. I didn't know anything about television or even advertising in general, so I failed miserably at the assignment. The good news is that I became intrigued with storyboarding and wanted to find out what it was all about. Years later, I understood that everything I did on that first storyboard was wrong. But I doubt if that ad agency ever learned its lesson about calling up artists at the last minute to produce drawings instead of creating a proper storyboard.

Every artist will have a first assignment. When you have yours, you will have read this book and will know that drawing a comic strip is not the same as creating a storyboard.

WHAT YOU NEED TO GET STARTED

Tools of the Trade

The tools needed to create a storyboard are very simple and inexpensive. This is one of those professions that requires little in terms of start-up equipment. To begin with, all you really need is a pencil, pen, and lots of paper. Oh, and perhaps most importantly, you'll need a good measure of dedication!

When I am working on the move, all I often have with me are a pen and paper. But here is a detailed list of supplies and equipment you will eventually want to own for your storyboarding work.

■ **Paper** – I recommend using the most common paper available on the market, plain copier paper. Plain copier paper is cheap, and that is important because you will need to buy paper in large quantities. And speaking of large quantities, it is best to buy paper by the ream or the case instead of purchasing small packages. Copier paper also comes in the convenient size of 8½" x 11" sheets. This paper size fits just about any scanner for reproducing illustrations and also fits in standard binders for filing. For certain jobs, such as production drawings or fine illustrations, you will need to use a better quality paper, but for most sketching and regular storyboarding, copier paper works fine.

■ **Pencils and Pens** – There are hundreds of choices when it comes to pens and pencils. The end result is basically the same for all of them. What is used is really up to the artist. All artists have their preferences. My recommendation is to obtain a large variety of pens and pencils and experiment using them with different styles and techniques. It's best to keep your pens and pencils in some sort of case so they are not easily lost or left behind when you are working away from home. If not a case, simply use a rubber band to bind them together.

■ **Markers** – Colored or gray-scale markers are very useful for storyboarding. A few shades can give a board a more professional look. In general, storyboards are done in black and white, but occasionally colors will be required. Graphic markers are the best choice for color because they immediately dry on paper and come in a wide range of tones and grades. The downside is that markers can be quite expensive, especially if you need to purchase a whole set all at once. Alternatively, you can choose to color boards on the computer.

■ **Computer** – The computer has become an essential tool in the life of the freelancer. I come from a time when the main computer on the market was the Commodore 64, and having a mobile phone was out of the question unless you happened to be wealthy enough to afford one of those brick-sized devices. Times have changed! Now, the computer has revolutionized people's lives, and this is true in my profession as well as so many others.

It doesn't matter whether you choose a Mac or a PC, as they both run the same programs for artists. You will not need to be a computer expert to storyboard, but you will need to become familiar with some programs and how to utilize them. Before you shop for a computer, do your research so you get a computer that is best suited for your profession. The focus of your investment in a computer should be based on graphics. This means that the monitor, the processor speed of the computer, and the RAM should be considered. Your computer should have a minimum four GB of RAM to run graphic software. One last note on computer usage: Make sure you can automatically back up and restore lost files, as well as recover the system in the event of a crash. This is standard on all new computers now, but you should be aware of this if you are planning on using an older computer for your work.

 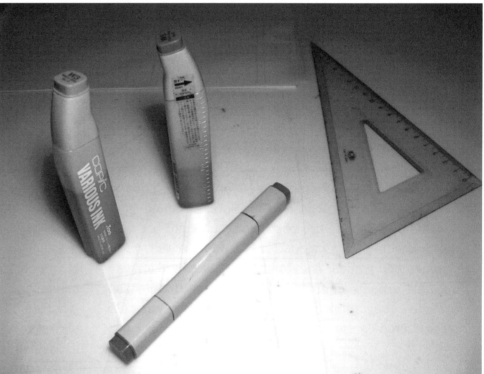

- **All-in-one Printer** – The all-in-one printer usually consists of a scanner, printer, copier, and card reader. This multi-purpose machine is probably the most practical solution for anyone who has a small studio. Because there is only one machine, it limits the number of wires and cables that must be plugged in and run across the floor, and you don't need space for several different machines. The all-in-one printer is affordable for one just starting out in the profession and has all the functions a storyboarder needs.

The quality of the scanner in an all-in-one printer is usually pretty decent. If you need to work with high-quality scans, you may want to invest in a separate scanner, but a resolution of 1200 dpi is more than adequate for storyboard work. The most important qualities in evaluating the scanner are that you need to be able to scan a few pages in just a few minutes, and to be able to immediately and easily use the software without a sharp learning curve. If you are eager to get to work, you won't want to have to endure several hours of tutorials just to use your scanner software for a simple project.

When you consider the printer, keep in mind the cost of the printer cartridges. While the printer is not a large investment, printer cartridges can be expensive, and it doesn't take long to go through one when you are printing graphics. Many all-in-one printers include a fax, but faxes are virtually obsolete and are not the best option for sending graphics. It is better to send graphics by e-mail so loss of resolution is avoided.

- **USB Flash Drive** – This is a compact, simple device that easily fits in your pocket and allows you to collect reference material from a client's computer. Files can be downloaded onto this tiny device, and then the material is available from any computer when you need it. This is handy because often graphic files can be too large to send via e-mail. As long as you have your USB flash drive with you, no worries.

- **Digital Camera** – I often use a digital camera to take reference pictures. The pictures can be used to remind me of details that I might otherwise overlook or forget. I have found many uses for the digital camera in my storyboarding profession, and no doubt you will, too. The digital camera is easy to use and there is no struggling with keeping up with film canisters and remembering to have film developed. In addition, you can quickly download pictures to your computer, edit them, and work with them in the program of your choice.

- **Light Box and Table** – The light table is a very important tool for the storyboard artist. The table you use should be the right height to be comfortable when you are sitting and working, and large enough so that you don't have to support your weight on your drawing arm when you are working. To avoid that, you will want to choose one that is larger than the A-3 format or a slim one like the one that is used by photographers for reviewing negatives and slides. You may consider building your own custom light table that perfectly suits your needs.

- **Binders** – Any sort of binder or folder works great for archiving storyboard illustrations or reference material. You can protect your illustrations by placing them in archival quality plastic sheet protectors before putting them in your binder. Your local office supply store will provide you with many alternatives for keeping your studio in order. Just keep in mind that moisture of any kind can ruin your illustrations, so store binders in a dry place.

- **Drawing Tablets** – Even though I am a traditional storyboard artist, I discovered the versatility and convenience of a good drawing tablet. There are simple small tablets that can be used when traveling, as well as highly professional, large-format tablets. A wide range of affordable tablets is available to suit the needs and preferences of any artist. One thing to keep in mind when choosing a tablet is that its cover will protect your illustrations while you are on the move.

- **Graphic Software** – There are several graphic artist software programs available. What you choose will depend on what type of projects you work on and what features you need. Because so many programs are available, you can quickly spend a small fortune on software that you find out later you don't need. Before choosing software, check online to see if you can download a trial version before purchasing the full version. Before you buy software, read the system requirements and make sure your system can run the software.

Going Digital

As a professional, I have always tried to keep up to date with the latest techniques to improve my work and expand my art. So whenever something new came out on the market, I simply saw it as an investment that would pay for itself in additional work. I was right. My investments in updated tools and equipment have always paid off.

Don't be afraid to purchase the newest tablet or whatever else you need if it is something that will improve your work and ease your workload. If the new tablet will be a tool that you frequently use or use for special purposes, buy it. Consider the fact that it will pay for itself with the additional jobs you can get. There was a time when I used my own "storyboard currency." When I spent money for a new tool or equipment for my work, I would say, "It will take two storyboards to pay for this tool." This method of accounting helped me maintain better control over my finances and helped me understand exactly what my new tools would cost me.

I don't follow trends, but I do try to take advantage of new technology that can improve my work. When I purchased a mobile phone, some of my friends thought it was too weird for a freelancer without a steady job to have a mobile phone. I taught myself how to use the computer, but continued to work mostly on paper. I used the computer to clean up drawings, scan the board, add colors, and so forth. But my use of the computer ultimately, by chance, led me to the digital drawing field.

It happened that I was traveling and, out of the blue, I received a call from an agency for which I had previously freelanced. I had absolutely nothing to work with except my laptop. It wouldn't have been a problem to find paper and pen, but the agency needed the storyboard ASAP, and I was at a further disadvantage because of the time zone that I was in. I had no time to spare! I immediately went to the closest office supply store to purchase something I could work on and that's when I noticed a digital drawing pad for sale. I thought that this might be a good time for me to give it a try. You may think it was crazy for me to experiment with a new tool at a time when I was on such a tight deadline, but I can be very efficient when under stress. (Note that I don't like that kind of stress and, after this incident, I made it a habit always to travel with a block and pens in my bag.)

I went back to the hotel and installed the digital tablet. It was absolutely my first time using a digital drawing pen. Fortunately, the installation was simple and successful and I could immediately practice using the features that I needed for my job. I have to admit that it was a difficult task for me, and as I worked I feared that I wouldn't be able to master the techniques and complete the job. I didn't give up, and before I knew it, I was pretty familiar with the new tool and finished the job. It wasn't a top-notch job, but considering the situation and the tight deadline, I think it worked out fine. Most importantly, the agency was satisfied with the work. Now, I wouldn't recommend starting a job using a new tool with which you haven't practiced. I also don't recommend that you get stuck in a rut and refuse to try new tools. I have met many artists who, on principle, will not try anything new. I believe that in refusing to try new tools, they are limiting the possibilities in their work.

Right now, I alternate between working on paper and on the computer, depending on the job and the situation at hand. I do a lot of my work on a digital tablet, which I find very useful, especially when I work away from my studio. When I am working in an ad agency office, the digital tablet allows me to work independently, without having to borrow copiers, scanners, or other items. I can remain focused on my work and not distract anyone, including myself. While working at home, there are many distractions to woo me away from my desk, but when I work at an ad agency office, I try to sit comfortably and remain focused.

There is a nice variety of software that can be used for drawing with the digital pen. My favorites are Sketchbook and Photoshop. I have used them for a long time and have learned the most important shortcuts to make my work faster.

The advantages of working with a digital tablet are numerous. With the digital tablet you have the ability to quickly and easily correct the drawings. Additionally, the tablet makes copying pictures much easier with the use of layers. And, by the way, you shouldn't be ashamed to copy from photos. This is an excellent way to improve your skills. What better way is there to learn to draw a car than by tracing it directly from a photo?

With a bit of experience, one can sketch out the storyboard and at the same time research pictures from the Internet to be used in the composition. Once the pictures are collected and the rough board is ready, those images can be mounted in a background layer, scaled and resized to fit the frame, and the intensity adjusted to make the tracing easier. After that, it is only a matter of patiently cleaning up the sketches and inking the board.

In the beginning, this procedure might prove to be tedious and time-consuming, but after a while you will be able to process the work according to your preferences.

There are several websites where you can search for and download images. Simply type "images" or "graphics" into your Web browser and you will see many sites that offer images suitable for freelancers. Sometimes the ad agency will provide you with reference material. In any case, it is a good practice for any artist to create a library of the most common images used. That way, you can also practice your digital pen skills when you are between jobs.

It is worth noting that some laptops allow you to draw directly on the screen. I believe this is the best solution for artists who are frequently on the go.

Of course, colorizing with a digital pen beats using a mouse (not to mention the fact that you can eliminate that irritating mouse-related pain known as tennis elbow). The digital pen is more natural, as well as quicker. The pen also allows you to add shadows and final touches to the illustration when working in gray scale, which is mostly what a storyboard artist does.

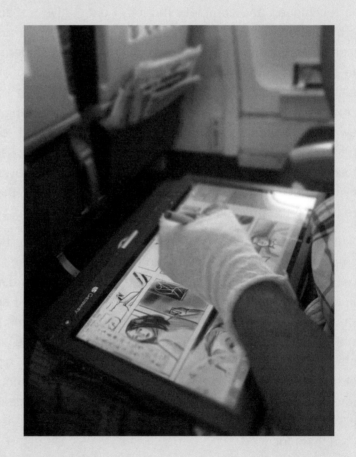

Sitting near the emergency exit on a plane gives you more legroom.

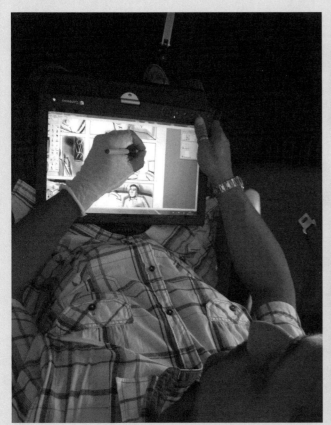  

It really doesn't matter how you apply the gray tone. In general, I don't follow any rule in particular, but I go by instinct.

It is on rare occasion that a storyboard artist must refer to the exact lighting on set. The lighting information, as well as the set design, are often not available during the storyboarding process, except when specified in the script, such as when a character is backlit. Other than that, the gray tone purpose is to embellish the frames and give them depth or to enhance certain details in the composition.

To give depth to a frame quickly, I usually add a first layer of light gray to the image, covering in the most obvious spot, but for the most part, I tend to fill almost the whole frame. Then I proceed with a darker tone that gives hints of shadows, and I finish with an even darker color to work on some details.

I worked out this board using the tablet, and I worked as if I were painting. I added layers of grays as I moved along with the work, usually starting with the darkest tone and adding details with lighter colors on the gray palette. Working digitally gives you a much easier and more immediate use of the white color. Note the street lamps or the reflection of light on the car where I used the airbrush tool.

STORYBOARD ARTISTS AND COMIC STRIP ARTISTS

I often have discussions with my colleagues about the differences in the work of comic artists and storyboard artists. In general, many people consider the storyboard as a comic book or script. This is not correct. Yes, the storyboard is a process that presents the script in pictures, but unlike with comics, there are many limitations and rules that storyboard artists must consider when doing their job.

Some artists would argue that it's easier for a comic artist to become a storyboarder than for the storyboard artist to work in comics. Perhaps this is true when considering only drawing skills, but for drawing storyboards, artists must have many other skills and talents. As an example, they must possess the ability to adapt to the director's style and transfer his or her vision onto the board. While maintaining the style and language of the project, the storyboarder must understand what is doable and what is impossible to achieve. The storyboarder understands that even one frame that varies from the set style and language can change the entire concept.

To be more specific, when storyboard artists are working on a board, they must be aware of what equipment will be available during the shooting. For instance, it wouldn't be right to draw a helicopter scene when there isn't one. In addition to considering the style and vision of the director, the storyboard artist must be able to look at how the scenes flow and work together, and what the end result will look like. All of this will affect the storytelling, as well as other elements of the film.

Another consideration of the storyboarder is the actual frame ratio. Whereas in comics artists can choose whatever framing they feel necessary to bring the story to life, in film artists have only one format and everything must adapt to it.

When you analyze the scripts provided for the comic or the storyboard, you will see that the structure of each is different. Comic scripts usually tend to be more detailed than film scripts when it comes to descriptions. In general, the comic artist has more liberty in choosing location, framing, timeline, and continuity. A storyboard artist must consider several important factors at all times, including the characters' motivation. The storyboard artist must somehow make the story believable and the events logical and consistent with the script, even if it means making suggestions for script changes at times.

In comics, the artist is the final creator of the work, but in filmmaking, the storyboard artist continues to manage the script and follow the instructions of the crew. The whole production often depends on the storyboard in order to calculate schedules, acquire funding, instruct crews, scout out locations, contact actors, revise the script, and so forth.

As the two examples demonstrate, the approaches to the works are completely different. The concerns of the artists are also different. For one, the continuity and the flow require different needs and schemes.

In the comic example, you will immediately notice how the page has been designed to give an overall impact by displaying the sequence on a single page, despite the characters' position in the scene. In fact, you can follow the story without getting confused about the direction because all the frames are displayed on the same page, whereas in the storyboarded version of the same action, you can immediately spot the differences. To start with, the female character is placed in the left frame of the comic and maintains that position throughout, providing a perfect geography of the scene. This is necessary because, if you look at the close-ups, you can refer to each character's position. For instance, frames 3 and 4 of the comic might be confusing as it isn't clear whether the characters are fronting each other.

Similarly, in frame 2, it is unclear whether the man has already turned. The continuity of the scene in the storyboard is constructed in a different manner than the comic page. It is more fluid and logical. When drawing the storyboard, the artist must also consider other kinds of production limitations, such as whether a crane shot should be considered for the opening scene. The comic artist is not responsible for choosing the framing to maximize the impact of the layout.

21

On the comic page, one must think of the overall impact, displaying the whole scene in a logical series of frames, while making sense of the script, whereas the storyboard sequence must answer a few other technical questions such as: Do we have a crane for the first introductive frame or establishing shot? Where is the line of action? What's the tempo of the scene? Of course, the examples can be executed in many different ways. A director might choose to shoot the scene in one take, but that's something that is discussed during the meeting and brainstorming sessions. One thing is certain, and that is the huge difference in style. Storyboarders never have the time that comic artists have to do their job. But that's fine, as many directors actually prefer the storyboard to look sketchy because the rough look of the picture enables the director to focus on the technical meaning of the board: what to shoot. A carefully drawn and inked storyboard (like a comic book) suggests that things are already settled, which may put clients or the producer on alert because they might think that that is how the film is going to look.

Most of all, a good storyboard artist should have a solid knowledge of film in order to provide the references — clips or scenes from other movies, style and techniques from other filmmakers, special camera movement, or new devices — that will be required from time to time. The storyboard artist should understand everything from film techniques, to choices of lenses and framing, to the capability of executing special effects.

The Artist Who Influenced Me

I started my profession working in the comics industry, first as a writer and then as an artist. I drew for various publishers, worked on my own scripts, and worked as a freelancer. At that time, I wasn't aware of the opportunity to work as a storyboard artist until I met one of my favorite artists, Jean Giraud, more widely known as Moebius. I had the good fortune to visit his home studio in Paris. While visiting, I took a close look at his work and, with a little bit of shame, I showed him my portfolio, which contained clones of his most famous work because I used to imitate his style. It was then that my eyes noticed something different on his desk. He was working on a storyboard and he explained to me what the frames were.

Jean Giraud had always been an innovative artist, and I realized how much work he had done for the movie industry both as a designer and storyboard artist. Yes, he was a comic artist and a storyboarder. He was also the artist who made a significant contribution to changing the comic world with his alter-ego artist, Moebius. He brought a completely new look and style to comics — one that, I believe, inspired an army of artists, including me.

That day, standing with this famous artist in his studio, I thought that perhaps I was in the wrong field. I didn't have my own style to begin with and "borrowed" from my favorite artists, but according to Giraud I had good storytelling skill and storyboarding was probably where I was going.

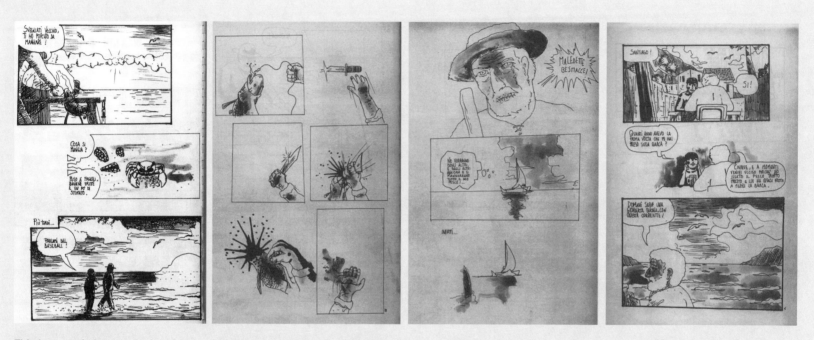

This is a comic I created when I was a kid. I used to read books and then make a comic version of them. I forgot about all the comics I had done, but my father kept them. He told me that one time they were showing the TV adaptation of the Hemingway book featuring Spencer Tracy, and he took out my comics and viewed them because they looked quite like the film. He said that some of the frames were almost the same as on the screen. I believe that the reason for this was that the book was very well written and the reader could visualize the scenes. I felt I could really see pictures of what was written. All I did was transfer it into drawing. And that is what a storyboard artist does in the end. I believe that was possibly my first attempt at creating a storyboard.

DRAWING SCHOOL

CHAPTER
4

The primary skill or talent you need to begin pursuing a storyboarding career is obviously drawing. However, I also intend this book to serve as a reference manual for people who are involved in the storyboarding process in some other capacity than as an artist. I wish to inspire young, talented beginners to try their hand at something they may never have heard of before, something that could become an exciting new challenge or profession.

So, while I am aware that not every reader who picks up this book has been practicing their drawing skills, I know that it is also clearly impossible to teach someone how to draw in one chapter. That is why I am giving you a crash course, sharing my personal tips on how to improve your drawing skills even if drawing is not your particular forte. Everyone can draw a little if they try — and that may be enough.

I have taught at many different schools and colleges over the years, and I sometimes give workshops at advertising schools where most of the programs focus on the writing rather than the visualizing. Consequently, drawing ability is not an essential prerequisite. Although some copywriters and art directors can do rough sketches of their ideas, you would be surprised to know how many of them have never even tried. For that very reason, my workshops usually require the students to team up and work together on a rough script or an idea to produce a storyboard. By the end of the day, everyone has completed their assignment, sometimes to their own surprise.

How can I make it any simpler? If you never try, you'll never know if you can do it. So pick up pencil and paper and start working on some drawings. You can begin by copying. There's no shame in that. Every artist has started out by copying someone else's work. It doesn't matter whether it's a photo or an illustration of some kind. Just get used to proportions and balance, but most importantly, accustom your hand to drawing.

I find that drawing silhouettes can help you gain confidence with proportions. Horses are particularly difficult creatures to draw, especially when the horse is in motion. My tip is to begin from a static position to learn the size and proportion of the different body parts. Once the location and structure of the body parts and movement are understood, it's much easier to reproduce the animal in motion.

Some people have a natural talent for drawing, whereas others have difficulty making their pictures understandable. Even rough doodles can help a director or copywriter when they are trying to explain what they want, making communication with the artist much easier. This is especially true when the focus is not on the quality of the drawing, but on the action that is taking place. For that is the very essence of storyboarding. You can draw a box with wheels and that can represent a car. You can draw arrows to show the direction and so forth. It's simple, and it's something that anyone can do, regardless of their draftsmanship.

One of the storyboard artist's skills should be to simplify drawings so they are down to the barest essentials. Since the artist has to be fast, most of the details in a frame can easily be left out. This will keep the viewer from becoming distracted by details that are not that important to the action taking place. Your main focus should be on the meaning of the frame and how it is going to be used. Basically, the storyboard artist should know what he or she needs to draw and focus only on that. Another reason to keep it simple is because many of the elements in a frame often have not been precisely determined yet. For example, the artist will often have to work on an action scene in an environment that has not been determined, so there is no point in designing something that may turn out to be completely different in the end.

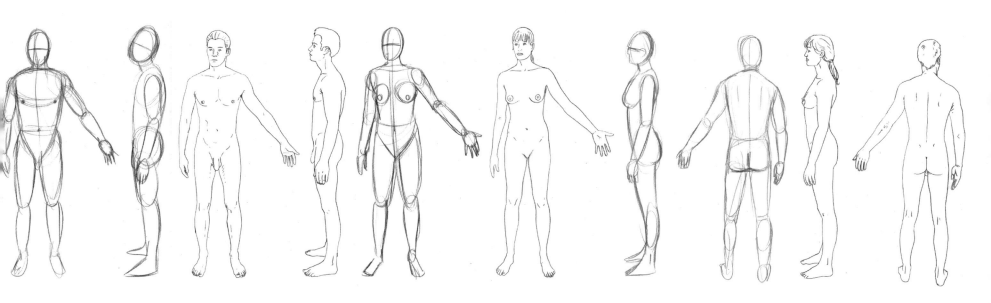

Understanding and Drawing Anatomy

Drawing people and understanding anatomy is probably a good place for an aspiring storyboarder to start. And since there are people all around us, probably the best advice I can give to an upcoming artist is to be a good observer and to get into the habit of carrying around a small sketchbook.

There are many ways to learn anatomy. One of the most common is to join a live drawing class. Art schools usually offer classes that even non-students can attend. Another option is to look for posts about art classes on the school bulletin board or on the bulletin board at art supply shops.

You can only learn about the human figure and movement by watching bodies and understanding how they move. Another good piece of advice is to get into the habit of using the digital camera to build a sequence which you can then reproduce in drawing form. As an example, ask a friend to do a series of rough movements as if you were going to draw a storyboard sequence of it. This is also a technique that you can use later on when you're actually working on a real storyboard. It simply makes things easier, and all artists use photographs as reference, so there is nothing to be ashamed of.

Copying is just one way of learning, possibly the best.

Knowing anatomy and being able to draw a human body is only the first step. You also need to know how real people look and move.

Bodies have different shapes and people dress in different ways, so practicing in your sketchbook while sitting in a coffee shop, in a waiting room, or at the railway station can help you widen your vision. You will soon discover that there is much to see and that you usually miss a lot of details because you don't really carefully look at things.

Copying from a magazine is another good exercise for practice. A photo may inspire a complete illustration or you just may want to reproduce the same image exactly as is. It doesn't matter as long as you practice.

A good artist should have a stock of what we commonly call "reference material" in the studio. Reference material primarily consists of magazines of any kind and on any topic: cars, sports, fashion. The magazines contain pictures that can be used as inspiration and to practice drawing. Tracing paper can be the perfect paper for tracing photographs. It can be bought in pads of various sizes, as well as in rolls, and is available in most art supply stores. Learn first how to trace just the essentials in a photo, that is, the basic form, in order to understand the construction of the image. A good exercise is to give yourself a time limit in which to reproduce the image. This will keep you from spending too much time on the picture and teach you to sketch quickly, just like you must do in live drawing sessions in art school.

Understanding Perspective

The second most important concept for an artist is perspective. Obviously, for the storyboard artist this is particularly vital.

To help understand perspective, nothing works better than using construction lines.

In the beginning, you will probably always have to refer to the lines. Don't worry: After a while it will start to become natural to draw objects in scale and properly placed within frame.

Understanding Framing

A common problem for beginners is learning how to frame correctly or, to be more precise, how to draw within a frame. For that you should learn to use construction forms or blocks. In other words, you have to learn how to sketch effectively. This is very important because sketching is essentially all you'll be doing during meetings with directors or art directors.

One of my favorite exercises is the one I call "sketching steps." Basically, you start with a very rough sketch, the most immediate you can come up with, draw freehand without focusing on anything except for the form and position. I recommend using a red or blue pencil because the next step will be made with a regular pencil, which will immediately become noticeable when the lines are drawn over the red or blue tones. Another reason is that the red and blue tone will not appear when you make a photocopy of it, or else it can easily be removed in Adobe Photoshop® or another software program. The next step is a quick clean-up of the previous rough sketch, going over the first lines you made and retracing the ones that appear to be correct or close to the image you want to produce.

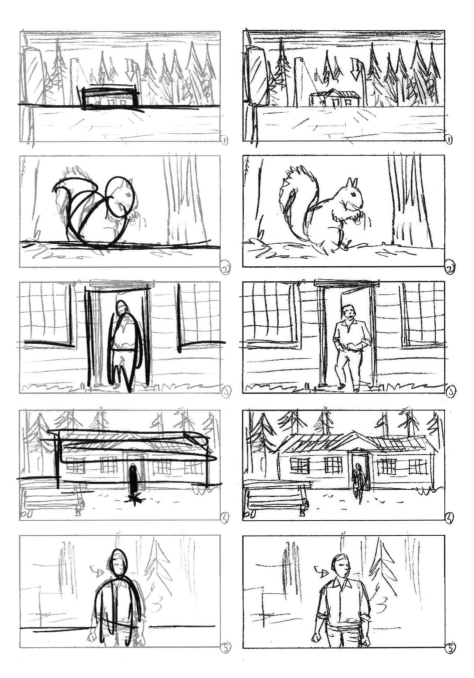

THE STORYBOARD ARTIST / Giuseppe Cristiano

Finally, move the work over to the light table and use a pen to trace the final illustration, which now has become more visible and detailed. I have counted three steps, but depending on the work you are doing, it might require more. For example, you can work on the background on a separate sheet or you can add another character later on. It all depends on your particular skills, and of course it requires patience, which is another talent a good storyboard artist needs to master.

Do you have a pet? Maybe you have a cat or a dog? Sketching your pet whenever you have a little time to kill can be a great exercise to help you develop drawing skills.

To get used to working in frames, a good exercise is to draw it and frame it later. Just draw any doodles or situations and then decide what the most interesting frame is. It's sort of the same principle as searching through the viewfinder of your camera for the right photograph to shoot. Directors often use their fingers to frame a scene. You might recognize the gesture from movies you've seen. Framing with the fingers is a way to isolate the space around what you are most interested in. Framing helps you to focus on certain details and to balance a frame.

Freeze frame on your player and get on with your sketchbook. It is a good excercise to help you understand framing and composition.

Have you ever taken a picture of a friend sitting at the beach or standing in a huge field of dirt or grass? When you look at the picture, you barely see the friend because of all the surrounding sand or grass. So you decide to "frame" your friend and crop the picture so the friend is the focus of the picture.

THE STORYBOARD ARTIST / Giuseppe Cristiano

THE STORYBOARD ARTIST / Giuseppe Cristiano

Technical and Camera Movements

To begin working with frames, you should first be aware of what sort of techniques are available or at least have a general grasp of what is possible to achieve with a camera. This is especially true when it comes to movement. Storyboarding is not simply about drawing a series of frames in a sequence. You must also justify the frames so they coordinate with the action to create continuity between the shots. Certain moments in the story require a particular kind of framing. The old cliché that a picture is worth a thousand words is true, and a storyboard artist would do well to keep that in mind when working on a board.

There are a series of standard framing alternatives that you should know by name, since they are the most common shots used in filmmaking. But, more importantly, you need to know when and how to use them.

Normally, a film will be shot keeping the camera at a horizontal aspect. Tilting the camera draws attention to the importance of the scene in some way. In fact, the choice of camera angle determines the mood of the scene.

LOW ANGLE SHOT is, in general, used to convey power, strength, and superiority. Often it is used to introduce characters. Just imagine the hero entering a room or the opening shot of an evil character and you will understand how this shot is used.

HIGH ANGLE SHOT gives the opposite effect of the low angle shot and is used to represent fear, inferiority, and less significant characters.

One important note I would like to make here is that these two particular shots are used together, one after the other, as if there were a dialogue or a conversation between shots. Imagine the situation of a male character entering a room in a low angle shot — he is powerful and strong, but over what and whom? That low angle shot will immediately be followed by a high angle shot, perhaps of the room, to reveal the danger or the situation, or perhaps a high angle shot of a character turning toward the threat that just entered the room.

The same observation can be made with a very typical situation that many horror movie buffs will instantly recognize: A camera is moving toward an abandoned creepy house, obviously in a low angle shot, to view the menacing mansion in all its threatening prominence. A typical following shot is the view down from one of the windows of the house (a high angle shot) revealing the courageous, but not very careful, characters who are walking toward the house. As you can see, both the shots are necessary and are linked together.

Before I move on to illustrate other framings, I want to take the opportunity here to stress how much a storyboard artist can learn from watching movies, especially the classics. In fact, I suggest that you build up your own little reference library. Try to get hold of the most important cult films and don't limit yourself to only the most common recent blockbusters. Look for movies by those pioneering maverick directors who paved the way for everyone who followed. For example, returning to our simple situation described above with the creepy house introduced in a low angle shot: Isn't that something you've seen before in *Psycho* by Alfred Hitchcock? In fact, not only was that infamous house in *Psycho* framed in low angle shots, but the house itself was built on a little hill to give it an even more threatening look.

After observing for a while, a storyboard artist will recognize the shots in films and almost be able to predict what the next situation will be, as well as understand certain visual fore-shadowing. This can ruin the intended surprise for the movie viewer. For that reason, the storyboard artist must be creative so as to avoid certain clichéd sequences. In the previous example, when movie viewers see the characters approaching the house from the view of the window, they know immediately that it suggests that something or someone is inside the house watching from the window, and that the characters may be in danger as they enter the house. If that is what the script has in store, we don't want to anticipate the action, so one solution might be to find another camera position that either doesn't reveal that there is a threat in the house (although we assume so) or that our characters are going inside (though we assume that too).

CANTED ANGLE SHOT, sometimes also called a Dutch Shot or Hong Kong Shot, is when the camera is tilted. This shot is often used as a cheap trick to speed up the action.

is when the camera is placed on a high vantage point over-looking a situation, but it can also be a or a , depending on the scene. In any case, it can be referred to as a HIGH ANGLE SHOT, to which we can then respond with a LOW ANGLE SHOT. For example, if we see a car screeching to a halt right outside a building framed in a BEW or TOP SHOT, one of our questions will be who's watching, (a) and in that case we might want to show the person in the window with a LOW ANGLE SHOT in order to balance our choices. Or (b) we could use the LOW ANGLE SHOT of the roof of the building, where a character is ready to jump, still in a LOW ANGLE SHOT. Or (c) we can intro-duce the characters who just arrived on the scene. In each case, we use a LOW ANGLE framing in response to the HIGH ANGLE of the BIRD'S EYE view.

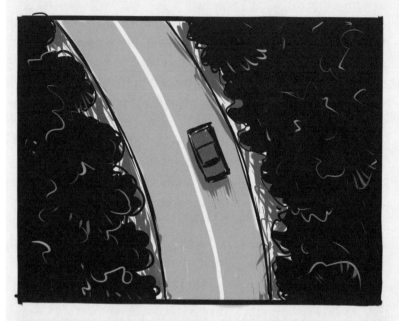

GROUND SHOT is achieved literally by placing the camera on the ground. The effect is that one loses the perspective since all the objects will be on the same horizon line. This was used very much in the seventies and in spaghetti westerns, and it works very well for confrontational scenes.

In order to capture emotions and emphasize action scenes, artists really need to read the script properly and make sure

they fully understand it. This may seem like an obvious point, but you'd be surprised how many times I've been called in by a director to work on a board done by some other artist

who has completely missed the intention of the script. It is important to understand what the actors will be doing in each scene, how they will act, and even to understand their emotional state in order to build up the intensity of the moment or justify a certain sequence.

A script generally will not (and should not) contain any references to camera angles, which are the responsibility and prerogative of the director and the cinematographer. However, the first version of the board is often left up to the storyboard artist to do on his or her own (especially in animation and advertising). So, just like a director, the storyboard artist has to "see" the film through the script. One good exercise that you can do to get used to translating a text into images, especially scenes, is to pick up pages from one of your favorite books and make a storyboard out of it, as if you were preparing for a shoot. This is how I learned how to do storyboards when I was a kid.

ZOOMING is simply represented by arrows in a frame.

e·on
ELECTRIC SCOOTER

Camera movements can vary depending on the equipment used, but the most common are **DOLLY SHOTS** and **PANS**. A DOLLY is a camera mounted on a wheeled platform, allowing it to take continuous shots in motion. It is represented on a board with arrows, but is also usually indicated in writing just to make it clear what the intention of the shot is. Simply called DOLLY SHOT, it can be in or out.

Do not be afraid to add arrows in the frames, as they are necessary to visualize direction and camera movements, and they make your board more dynamic and readable.

THE STORYBOARD ARTIST / Giuseppe Cristiano

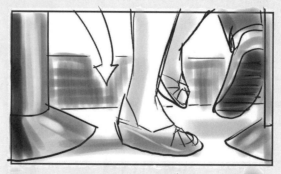

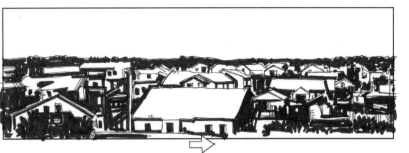

Sometimes when drawing a pan, it can be a good idea to reproduce the action in one long frame. You can see an example of this in this photo.

PANNING is achieved when rotating the camera on its axes.

PAN and **DOLLY SHOTS** can be combined.

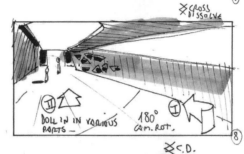

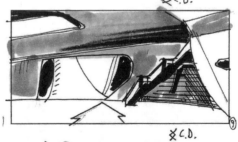

This is a storyboard produced for a completely different medium: a visualization for an architect's studio. The clients were working on the realization of a new important art museum and they needed to produce a dynamic 3D-animated film. Since the structure of the building was organic, they wanted a film with a lot of camera movements, mostly from the visitor's point of view. Therefore, several combined shots were used, such as a combination of camera dollys and pans.

STEADICAM is a stabilizing mount for cameras that allows for a smooth shot. The STEADICAM was invented by American filmmaker and inventor Garret Brown and introduced to the film industry in 1976. One of the first major breakout movies that used the STEADICAM was .

PLAN SEQUENCE is obtained by filming a scene continuously without interruption and can be achieved by using various devices. For example, a planned sequence could be done as a STEADICAM shot as well as a DOLLY SHOT.

CRANE is a mechanical arm to which a camera can be attached, allowing shots of great impact. As I mentioned before, studying the classics gives an artist a solid background that can often be used as a reference and as a basis for innovation. Take the CRANE SHOT in the dancing scene of , for example. It's easy to see what a reference it has become for the many films that came after it.

It's important to be aware that many cinematographers create their own devices to achieve certain shots, often because of budget limitations or because the necessary equipment has not yet been developed to film the very original and impressive scene. Therefore, it can be very useful for the director of photography to be present during the storyboard brainstorming session.

Distances

EXTREME LONG SHOT is a shot in which you have a huge land-scape but no focus on what the scene is about. An example might be an opening shot for a documentary scene where you provide a general impression of the environment, but you haven't yet really introduced the topic.

MEDIUM LONG SHOT uses a closer frame in which you start noticing elements that might be part of the story. At the same time, you are still too far away to determine who and what the topic of your documentary or story is.

LONG SHOT, also called a **MASTER SHOT** or an **ESTABLISHING SHOT**, is the moment when you finally frame the subject of your story. The ESTABLISHING SHOT is a very important frame in a story. Have you noticed that no matter how many episodes there are of *The Simpsons*, each time you enter the Simpsons' house, the school, or any other familiar location in the series, you still see the exterior shot of each place. This is the ESTABLISHING SHOT, the frame that tells what the location is. That is because there will always be someone who is watching the show for the very first time. The same procedure is true of TV series in general. The audience always needs to understand where you are going.

In feature films, the order of the shots can be inverted to introduce the element of surprise. In fact, it is often much more interesting not to reveal where you are all of the time, since you are telling the whole story in one film anyway and don't have to account for several episodes.

FOLLOW SHOT is when a camera follows a subject. The camera can be mounted on a dolly or vehicle or any other device. It is represented, once again, with an arrow.

In general, it is customary to add notes and write text on the storyboard frames as long as the text doesn't attempt to explain the whole picture. There is nothing more annoying than being confronted with a long paragraph of explanatory text when you're dealing with what is meant to be a visual medium. Certainly, no one is going to read the text anyway. The whole purpose of storyboarding a script is to visualize it as closely as possible to what the final filmed sequence will look like. Sometimes it is used to find new investors for the movie, in which case the whole board needs to be very clear. If text is really needed to understand your work, you've got a problem.

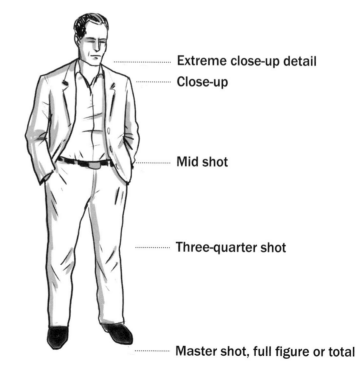

Extreme close-up detail

Close-up

Mid shot

Three-quarter shot

Master shot, full figure or total

Line of Action

At this point, it is essential to introduce the 180-degree rule, which is perhaps the most important basic principle in film-making. Essentially, for the 180-degree rule, imagine a line passing through two characters involved, for instance, in a dialogue scene. This imaginary line is called the line of action. The action in this case is the dialogue. Using the line, you have determined a 180-degree space within which the camera will be placed.

Now, take three different shots of the characters: A, B, C.

Using the line of action, you have established the positions of your characters. The guy is located on the left of the screen, and will remain so whatever the framing and no matter which position the camera takes up within that space. The line of action is there to help you avoid confusion during shooting. For example, if you frame a close-up of the girl "crossing" the line of action (frame D), you get confused since she is now looking in a different direction than where you thought the guy was positioned.

180°   LINE OF ACTION

A

B

C

This is a typical, very basic mistake that can actually be found in many films. And that's one of the annoying aspects of being a storyboard artist — that you often find yourself getting distracted because you are so acutely aware of any mistakes that crop up in the film.

In order to make it easier to keep track of the line of action, directors and cinematographers often draw floor plans of the set on which they note all the camera positions necessary for the shooting.

D

CUTAWAY SHOTS are, of course, not noted in the script and can be a perfect solution for editing. They come in very handy when the original shot cannot be used for some reason or another. Let's look at a simple example: An actor is talking to another character and he is holding a pen while doing his monologue. The dialogue is divided into various shots, and the actor switches hands in the different takes without anyone noticing, so in the two shots the pen has changed hands and therefore cannot be edited together. One of the shots has to go, unless there is a CUTAWAY SHOT that could be used in between. The CUTAWAY SHOT may be a reaction shot of the other character.

MATCH CUT can be used when your character is driving the car and suddenly he hears something from the radio. From a close-up of his car stereo, you cut to a radio in another environment. This is another solution that is never written in scripts and is left to the imagination of the artist or the intuition of the director.

Improve Your Style and Technique

Style and technique are your professional weapons and signature. You will be recognized and often chosen for your style, and it is advised that freelance artists adopt and develop a few different styles for different occasions that can arise. In the case of animation, the artist obviously needs to pick up the style of the show for which he or she has been hired. This is a completely different scenario, but when it comes to advertising, movies, and most other media, there is often more artistic freedom. A particular production will have its own preferences, and having a variety of styles to utilize will improve your chances of getting selected for the job.

Since the most common choice, especially when it comes to advertising, is to go for an artist who is capable of drawing realistic figures, it can be very useful to practice copying from photographs.

EXERCISE: Ask a friend to pose for you, build a sequence using your digital camera, print out the frames, and redraw them using your light table. Simplify the frames, concentrating on the form and composition more than the details.

It can be a very good idea to use comics as a reference when learning how to draw stylized and effective images. In the real workplace, you will typically be working against the clock, so it is essential that you master the ability to focus on the most important aspect of a picture with the least amount of effort.

Adding shades to your illustrations makes the pictures look richer. You can use markers as well as the computer for this purpose, whatever is more convenient.

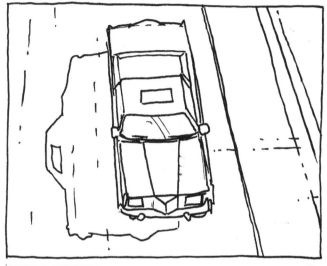

USE THE STORYBOARD AS A BUDGET

I touched on this subject in an earlier chapter, but I want to offer a little more detail here and stress the fact that the storyboard can serve as a valuable production tool. Understanding this can help you pitch your freelance storyboarding services, letting the production companies know that you understand all the benefits of a storyboard, not just the benefits of using it as a tool for shooting the movie.

On many occasions, I have explained to my students how a storyboard should be viewed as a necessary production tool, rather than simply as an illustrated script. In fact, I would go so far as to say that the storyboard can be used as a budget tool. The storyboard can be used to make rough calculations of the time and money that will be necessary to complete the project. You can estimate how many days will be needed for shooting and production, how many different sets and locations are required, how many people will be in the shots, what type of transportation is needed, what kind of equipment will need to be rented, what the daily shot list will be, and so forth. From there, using the storyboard, a timeline for the makeup sessions can be created, and even the number of lunches needed for the crew can be counted. As you can see, a wealth of information can be provided from the storyboard!

It is not only the completed storyboard that provides information, but the storyboard is useful even during brainstorming sessions or while the work is in progress. As you sit with the director and work through the script, you often discover that sections of the script don't really work as written. Perhaps there are scenes that can be rearranged to give the storyline a better flow or make a few changes that significantly improve the script.

It's quite normal during a brainstorming meeting for a director to start reworking the dialogue of a script to better fit the rearranged scenes. By the end of the meeting, you may find that you've ended up cutting ten to fifteen scenes from the script altogether. This can easily translate into a few days' less shooting time, representing a substantial savings in time and money (often one and the same in production).

Postproduction is often a very expensive step in filmmaking. The typical phrase, "We'll fix it in post," can easily turn the budget into a nightmare. For that reason, the focus of the storyboard, in some cases, should be on counting and analyzing the effects shots in the film, and determining what will have to be created in postproduction. Thus, a good amount of detail in the board will make the evaluation much easier, and the producer will certainly be much happier.

3A

3B

TILT UP

4A

Boss

4B

5

THE STORYBOARD AND ADVERTISING

It's quite likely that the advertising world will provide the first opportunity for a beginning storyboard artist to gain experience. It is potentially one of the main sources of income for a freelance artist, and it is not particularly difficult to gain entry. The most important aspect of this particular sector of the business is that it is very fast-paced and, consequently, you really have to be up to date and knowledgeable about what goes on in the industry.

One way to get to know the scene is to read industry magazines. The magazines feature various production companies and what they specialize in. You can become familiar with industry terms and find out the latest industry news by reading magazines. You can also visit specialty sites and databases on the Internet that provide the freelance artist with information on companies that are active.

There are various freelance artist organizations where you can network online or in person with other artists. Networking with other artists helps you stay caught up on what's what in the industry. Another advantage of networking is that it can sometimes lead to getting work through referrals from other artists who know and respect your work.

Advertising Agencies and Production Companies

In advertising, the phone call can come from an agency or a production company, and sometimes the same job can lead you from one to the other. The approach to the job will be different depending on which type of company contacts you, but in both cases a meeting will be required.

With advertising agencies, most of the time the job is progressive. Sometimes the same project will require several sessions and upgrades. Of course it depends, to some degree, on the campaign and how many people are involved, but in general the artist will only deal with the creative team. At a production company, the artist will work almost exclusively and very closely with the director.

When working with an advertising agency, most of the information is not immediately available. For example, the locations will likely not have been determined at the start of your job, as that is not essential to the agency's work, which mainly consists of developing the concept. However, once the project moves on to the production company, the practical details become very important and it is not unusual for the meeting with the artist to be put on hold until the locations have been approved.

The work with the production company requires more precision when it comes to the technical side of the shooting. Anything is allowed at the advertising agency stage, even complicated special effects that the agency may not yet know whether it can afford.

Client Boards and Shooting Boards

Every time I receive a phone call for a job, I always ask if the storyboard is for a client or a shooting board. Each kind of board requires a different approach. The main difference is that the client board should focus on conveying the spirit and content of the film, while the shooting board doesn't need to have such an accurate drawing style, but will need to be more precise when it comes to the technical aspects of the shooting and all that goes with it. Sometime this is a language that a client wouldn't understand, or worse, might even .

It is always better to avoid any complication when presenting the idea to a client, and sometimes the description of a certain camera technique would simply raise other questions that will distract the agency and the director from the job. Someone once told me that the best way to work on a commercial is to keep the client off the set. On one job, the clients insisted on visiting the studio where we were shooting a video. I had to give them the address, but I "accidentally" gave the address to another studio on the other side of town, so that I would have the time to shoot everything I needed before they realized the error. When they finally did show up, I was pretty much done with everything, and ended up having to spend most of the time explaining why the background I was shooting in the studio was just a green surface, instead of the one they had seen in the presentation.

From the examples in the figure on the preceding page, you can immediately see that, in the client board, the series of frames are only there to tell a story without going into details. The client board shows just the essence of it. I have drawn the so-called KEY FRAMES, which are basically the most important moments in the script. How you get to those frames is not important at this stage, and the way the director ultimately decides to shoot those scenes may look very different and adopt a completely different framing than was used in the client board. In the client board there is no continuity, and sometimes when I work with agencies I am asked to draw one to three frames that they will use only to explain the idea to the client. The shooting board, by contrast, contains everything that the director and crew need in order to actually make the film. Often, more shots are drawn than are needed, so that the director will have several alternatives for telling the story. Sometimes the director is not quite sure about certain shots, but will shoot them anyway and wait until the editing to decide whether to include them or not. But for the most part, what is drawn on the board is what is filmed.

Let's analyze the two boards and understand the various shots.

The shooting board is the main reference on a shoot. The frames will be pasted on a board, and, as the filming proceeds, they will be crossed out. A production assistant will

mark each of them, taking notes and collecting information that will be used to edit the film. The storyboard is definitely a useful tool for keeping track of the work-in-progress, considering that the shots are usually not taken in their logical sequence.

In this simple sequence, the director might choose to start with the wide shot, and since the lights are already in position, why not film the last shot, too? Right afterwards, since the actor is ready, you would move to the close-ups, followed by the over-the-shoulder with the girl, and concluding the whole sequence with the close-up of the girl.

This is how your storyboard is finally going to end up on a set. Cut into frames, pasted out on a black board, notes written all over the frames. Terrible, isn't it?

What Else Does a Storyboard Artist Do in the Advertising Business?

Not many people know that a storyboard artist often designs and illustrates ads and poster campaigns as well as events. Basically, the artist is called in during brainstorming sessions to help visualize all of the ideas generated by the agency so that the various teams can decide what to use for the client presentation.

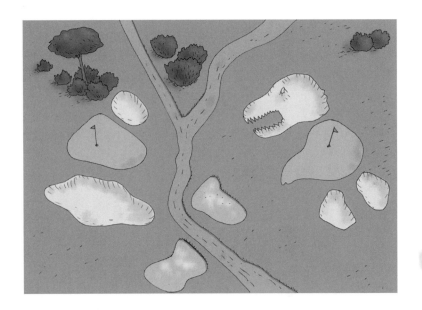

When an agency is planning an advertising campaign or some kind of public relations event in the city to advertise a product, the artist will be asked to illustrate the process. It might be a simple illustration showing, for example, a stand in the middle of a square, but nevertheless, it will be drawn. Once I drew a hamburger, just a plain, simple, sketchy one so that the agency could work out a rough layout for a campaign. The artistic team even asked me to write in the caption by hand, because they wanted to give it that work-in-progress feel so as not to stress out the client.

Of course, they could have used a stock image, but then the layout would have seemed finished, perhaps creating a sense of conclusion, and the clients might have felt pressured to sign or might have misjudged the work as already completed, as if they couldn't have the last word. Also, a drawing doesn't have the resolution of a photo so there wouldn't be any discussions about color, quality of the hamburger, size, ingredients, and so forth.

When I sketch designs for billboards, sometimes I give clients the option to orient the frame either as a portrait or landscape. I do that because they might want to consider a different size for the bill-boards, and it will just be easier if, in general, I draw the picture's canvas quite large so that they can crop the image for their purposes.

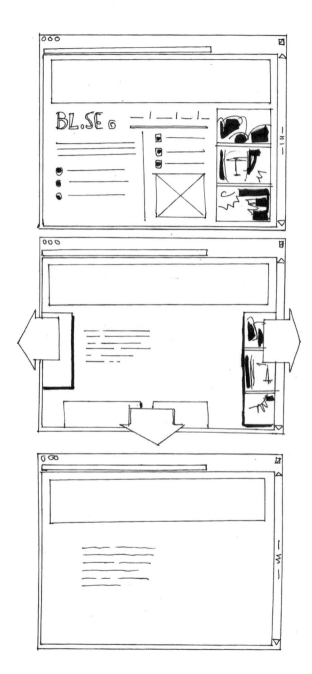

Another interesting reason why illustrations are used instead of stock images is that sometimes the agency doesn't want to give the client the idea that it is too eager to get the job, and an overly polished presentation might give that impression. So I have been asked by art directors on a number of occasions to keep my sketches rough and not to put too much effort and detail in my work right off the bat. Cushy work, huh?

It's not unusual for a storyboard artist to be called in to design websites and banners. It's a quite common assignment from advertising agencies these days, as the Internet has become such an important medium.

Events are special happenings planned by agencies that often have to be organized in public places, such as at a fair or a conference or a sponsorship event of some kind. For example, a certain brand might have decided to sponsor an important tennis tournament, in which case the clients would take the opportunity to promote themselves at the event with a stand and banners. In that case, the artist will have to illustrate how the client will be visible to the public at the event. Working almost like an architect, the artist has to plan out the tournament and the structures that will be used later on for the sponsor's advertising. Sometimes the work is not very accurate, since at the time of the planning there are, as yet, no blueprints or maps of the area because the event may be months away and the venue may not have even been selected. In that case, everything is left to the artist's imagination. It doesn't matter how close to reality the work is as long as it gives a general idea of what it's going to look like and how it's going to work.

At another time, you may need to illustrate how the events will take place, and the storyboard will become a description of the various phases, a sort of comic book of what will happen at the event. For example, the participants of the big conference will be greeted at the airport and then taken to the hotel where they will receive instructions for the following days. Each one of them will receive a USB key with the program. They will go to the conference which will be followed by a lunch. The illustrations will then be added to the PowerPoint presentation of the general idea and planning of the event.

A long time ago, I was approached for a very different kind of job. A company was working on the development of a new ride in an amusement park and it needed all sorts of artwork to present to the client in order to discuss the project.

Be Up to Date!

It is very important for professional artists to know what's happening within the field. You should know what new developments are taking place, what the different agencies are doing, what and even who has won awards and for what. Nowadays, thanks to the Internet, it's easy to keep up to date with everything. A plethora of information is just one

click away and it's free. However, I still always recommend that you acquire a reference library of books and material to have around in the studio for reference and inspiration.

There are special publications focused on various aspects of the industry, for instance, the advertising industry, that you might want to subscribe to in order to keep track of what's going on and to familiarize yourself with all the names in the business. Knowledge is important in this field, even though you might raise an eyebrow wondering why. It's just a matter of drawing pictures, after all. Right? Well, that's where you're wrong! This business is not just about drawing pictures, but about what those pictures say.

Commercials often refer to images with which people are already familiar. As an example, a commercial may emulate the style of a popular reality show or TV series. Or the commercial may parody popular public characters or celebrities. Some-

times commercials simply use language or a specific phrase that appeals to a certain target group. Therefore, it only makes sense to keep your eyes open to what's happening around you, absorbing all those visual references for future use. Find out what is cutting edge, what is popular with various groups, and what changes are on the horizon. Be informed. Be aware.

I once worked on a music video presentation, and the director had no idea who the band was. He didn't do any research, and even though I had their records, he insisted on a preconceived idea that he devised without bothering to find out anything about the band's world. Naturally, the project failed for that very obvious reason. It was clear that the director was not cut out for this kind of work and was taken off the job. All he would have needed to do to come up with some appropriate ideas was take the time to listen to the band's music and show some basic curiosity about the band.

Staying abreast of new techniques is also a plus for an artist, especially when working with directors. If you can speak their language, they will love you and want to work with you even more. You can open many doors if you are informed and willing to do a little research.

Movie magazines also provide pretty good reference material. I often end up in long conversations about movies with directors. Therefore, a good storyboard artist needs to watch lots of movies and has to be sure to remember the titles, directors, actors, and their works. Obviously, directors like their work and talking about it creates a connection. Of course, you have to be sure to check out the latest crop of movies. It always makes a good impression when you start talking about a newly released movie that the client or director hasn't seen yet.

Working with Ad Agents and Copywriters

When doing a job for an advertising agency, a storyboard artist primarily works with art directors and copywriters, except where fees and payment are concerned. All issues regarding invoicing should be discussed with either the project manager or the producer, as the art director or copywriter will have no idea about your fees.

It is good practice, once you've had the initial meeting for a job you're being hired to do, to have a quick chat with the production manager to make sure that he or she is aware that you have been brought on board, what work you're going to be doing, and, of course, how much you're expecting to be paid. This will help prevent a phone call from terrified agency members in response to the invoice you sent after spending the weekend producing a huge number of illustrations for them. It happens quite often that the creative team and the producer don't communicate enough about the work they have hired the artist to do. I have had to renegotiate my fee after a job was finished because of some misunderstanding regarding my fee.

Nevertheless, producers are not interested in details, so all you have to do is tell them your price list and they will check to see if that sounds doable for the budget they have calculated. Art directors are in charge of the visuals, while the copywriters produce the text. They work as a team, but sometimes the artist will only meet with one of them. It doesn't matter, since they work closely together and are in constant contact throughout the day. So don't be surprised if you send your work to one and receive comments from someone else you haven't even met. It happens quite often.

Some creative clients, such as art directors and copywriters (referred to as "creatives" in the industry), do rough sketches of their ideas, which is really useful during meetings. All you have to do at that point is translate their doodles into illustrations, adding your competence in framing and composition.

Other times they have a list of suggestions for illustrations, and for a campaign, they might want a large number of pictures to be produced for the next day. In that case, before you leave the agency, you really have to make sure that there is a budget for all the work you're being asked to do.

Depending on the relationship you have with the creatives, sometimes you might not even need to meet. Everything is done via e-mail, but that only works if you already have a well-established working relationship with the agency so it trusts your work. The best way to establish a relationship that allows you to work remotely without setting a meeting is to become very fast so you can complete a lot of sketches in a short period of time; also, make sure to respond to the creatives' e-mails promptly. That way, they will learn that distance work takes much less time than meeting in their offices to work out the sketches, depending on the mobility of the artist and location of the agency.

Usually, everyone is in a hurry in the advertising world, but don't be frightened by crazy requests. If they say they need it now, it simply means that it would be great if they could have it now. It's always negotiable and you can extend a deadline within reason.

Once I had to produce more than sixty frames for a pitch presentation and the agency absolutely wanted the work delivered within the next two hours because they were already late and they had to put together everything for the presentation. I simply explained to them that two hours wasn't enough time to do what they wanted me to do. Producing sixty illustrations in 120 minutes meant that I would have had to produce one illustration every two minutes, which is physically impossible. When I put the numbers down on paper, they realized that their request was impossible to fulfill, and the deadline was pushed back to the next morning. I still had to work all night to get it done, but at least it was doable.

From Idea to Treatment

Sometimes the creative team of an agency will want the artist to show up for some of the sessions at the agency in order to update the work-in-progress. This often involves spending the entire day, or more, at the agency to be on call to work on the sketches whenever necessary. It is not a common way of working, but since a lot of creatives are not very skilled at drawing, the doodles they make as they work through the project might be difficult for the other teams involved to understand. So they bring in the artist to clean them up.

In a way it is more of a convenient solution than a necessary one. Most of the work produced will never be used and will most likely be canned as the work-in-progress proceeds. To begin with, for such an assignment the artist should be prepared for long pauses between drawing sessions. This means that while the creative team is putting together its work or ideas, the artist might just be hanging around the agency cafeteria. These moments will then alternate with stressful sessions with people constantly coming up with sketch requests. I suggest that you take along something else to work on while you're waiting or bring something to read.

For artists who work on a computer, I suggest that you take along your laptop so you won't have to use one of the agency's computers. Remember, even though the team works with images, you cannot be sure that you will find the programs you are familiar with. Make sure a scanner is available; this will make your work so much easier, especially if you have to repeat frames or do quick adjustments.

With this kind of assignment, it is always good practice to discuss the financial side of the job with the producer. Basically, find out what the budget for the artist is in order to avoid an underpaid performance. Sometimes, the producer might suggest a flat fee rather than pay for the amount of work you actually do. This can end up being a bad deal for you if the work turns out to be much more than you anticipated. In one such assignment, I came close to producing one hundred illustrations over the course of the day, which didn't add up to very much per frame in the end. Negotiate your fee and be aware, more or less, of the amount of work necessary.

Occasionally, the artist might be asked to sit in for the brainstorming session, which mostly happens if the creatives want to hear the opinion of someone outside the agency. In that case, they welcome any suggestions you might have. Often, the artist will be better equipped to spot the weakness of an idea than the creatives are. Other than that, the artist gets fed, here and there, for the pictures and sketches that plaster the walls of the meeting room.

Often, the composition of the illustrations as well as the proper continuity of the board is left to the knowledge and talent of the artist. It can be very constructive, and indeed greatly appreciated, for the artist to suggest references, images, or films that might inspire ideas during the meeting. This can do much to elevate the storyboard artist's reputation, which is another reason always to be on the lookout for new films and inspirational material that can come in handy in this kind of situation.

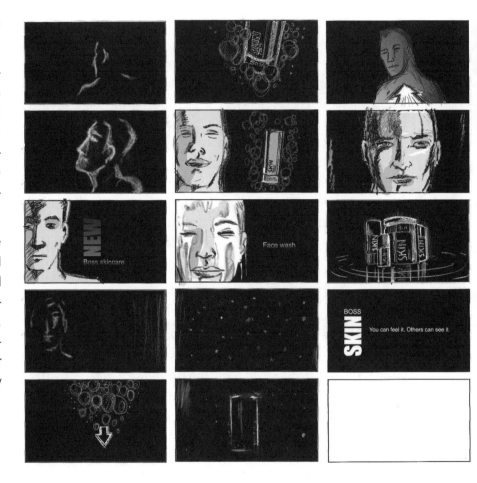

Brainstorming

When an artist is asked to meet with creatives at the agency, it doesn't mean that the idea or concept for the commercial or campaign is lying on a desk ready to be sketched. In many cases, the art director and copywriter are hoping for further input that the artist can provide during the meeting. They often ask the artist's opinion, and in some cases even test it on him or her to check whether the idea works.

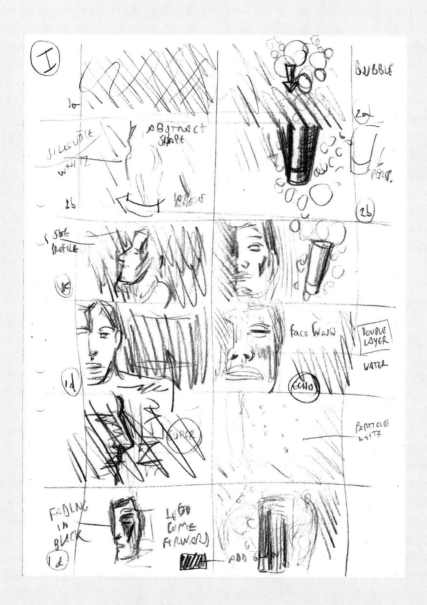

The input they are hoping for is purely creative. Sometimes they count on resolving problems that surfaced during their own sessions. They feel that a third person, someone outside of their office, might be the perfect mind to involve in the brainstorming. After all, the artist will work with the board or the poster concept, and his or her experience will help them to see things from different angles.

The meetings are generally fairly short, and maybe the artist has already been briefed by e-mail with a general overview of the project. Nevertheless, during the meeting the team will introduce the product or the client to the artist in order to understand what the purpose of the campaign is. After years of experience in the field, a professional artist will know all the various brands quite well, and what the focus of each job should be, and most importantly, what the character of each client is. This is important because there will always be so-called "difficult clients" to take into account from time to time.

Some clients get labeled "difficult" because they are more demanding or can't make up their mind, but sometimes the clients are only difficult because the agency doesn't know how to deal with them or the agency gives them more clout than they should. For example, the agency may allow clients to intrude into aspects of the work where they have no business being. A good client is one that trusts the expertise of the agency, but when there is a lot of money at stake, it can be difficult to set limits on the client's involvement. In such cases, artists can sometimes act as a sort of mediator or moderator of the idea, telling the creatives their point of view and bringing the work to a level of feasibility because sometimes the creatives don't know what is possible with the technique and they might promise too much to the client. One of the "tricks" in this case is to show them as little as possible, drawing only key frames, and leaving out the precise details of technical solutions that will ultimately be used. This reduces the time wasted on unnecessary discussions with clients, and frees up directors to choose whichever solutions they feel will work best during filming.

Sometimes an agency will ask for a client board in color. But in my experience it's best to avoid color when working on a clothing brand commercial, and leave this stage to the production company that will handle the film later.

During the brainstorming session, artists have to be quick in suggesting ideas for the visuals, but their main job is to translate into frames the agency treatment or script, although in many cases there is no script, just an idea. This results in the artist becoming a sort of director, which is why I always recommend learning the technique and language of film, in addition to gaining a wider awareness of what goes on in television and in movie theaters. Such references are vital for the advertising world.

Formulas and Strategies

When you have been working for so many years doing storyboards for advertising, you will start to recognize certain recurring patterns in the job. Much of your work will become routine.

To begin with, some products require specific shots. With the so-called product shots, you sometimes have to build a sequence in order to avoid the "right-in-your-face effect." The product shot should be casual. It shouldn't be evident or too aggressive. Sometimes, the product shot might appear only at the end of the commercial, but in commercials such as typical car commercials, the product might be all over the film. Some directors aren't very happy about placing product shots in "their" films, which they are dedicated to and treat like a short movie. But the client may think more like a salesperson and want the products to be featured as much as possible in the film. That is the reason that, at times, the shooting board might be unusually detailed in order to make perfectly clear where and how the product will be visible.

Some clients, the very big ones, have precise directives for the production companies. They have check lists and rules specifying how their products should look. And, in a worst-case scenario, they may already have a completely outdated packshot, or product shot, ready, which they have used before.

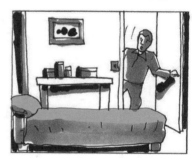

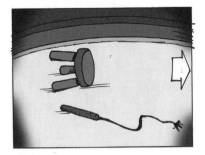

One bit of advice is to learn how to draw product packs as close as possible to how they look in reality. It will please the client.

In such a situation, the director might try to convince the client to shoot a new packshot in the style of the film, but otherwise, since the client already has the footage, there is no other option but to use it and adapt the rest to it.

Sometimes the artist feels like a train rolling along on tracks that can do very little other than follow client instructions and visualize the job through that perspective. This can be very frustrating and unchallenging for artists, and then the result is a sloppy job. The only solution to prevent that is to have a tight deadline; at least it works for me because that itself is a challenge. For artists, the real motivation is not the paycheck, but to improve style, skills, and outcomes. But that is something that producers are better not informed about, wouldn't you agree?

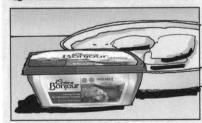

In the event of special products that are not yet available on the market, the artist should get a sample of the product or a work-in-progress picture of the packaging in order to avoid having to rework the board a second time. Once, I was told that a new soda drink package produced by a certain company was a small bottle, which I included almost everywhere on the board. After delivering a client board in full color, the design arrived, and it was a tetra pack instead. The whole board was completely useless. Information is important, so don't feel embarrassed to ask a lot of questions. Asking questions will save you time and will save the company time and money. Even if the clients act a bit annoyed about the questions in the beginning, in the end they will be glad that you bothered to gather as much information as possible before starting the storyboard.

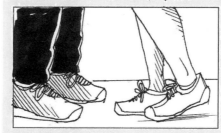

One of the most complicated situations for a storyboard artist is when asked to choreograph a certain action like a dance routine. In many cases, the artist will not even have music as a reference. I suggest focusing mostly on key frames and certain actions that the director might particularly like, and leave the sequence quite open. The framing, the close-ups, and the way the director wants to build the scene are more important than the action in these cases. Let the choreographers do the job unless they are present and able to give instructions during the initial meeting. It's not unusual, in fact, for the choreographer to be present during some of the storyboarding meetings.

If you are uncertain about a shot, my suggestion is to be vague in your work. In other words, don't fill up the frame with details that you may have to redraw. Focus on the main action and then you can revise later when you have more information. For example, in the picture to the left, the character is drinking a brand new juice, but you haven't gotten the packaging yet. Chances are that the juices have all the same pack form, so a mid-shot that is wide enough to see the action (man drinking juice) is enough for the purpose. The package will be just a small item in the frame that can be reworked during the revision stage, using layers where the correct layout can be added on the package.

I have often worked on clothing company commercials for which the agency didn't have the product list defined or the latest client choice available. In those cases, I always insisted on not creating a finalized board until the list was ready. As far as production was concerned, the meeting sketches were perfect for proceeding and it was easier for me to upgrade the board while the work progressed.

Perhaps the most challenging boards are the ones featuring cars since clients can be very picky about their cars and they know every detail of how the car looks. One of the most typical problems in a client board featuring cars is the color of the

car. In general, the agency will ask the artist to work the car using discreet colors that won't bring out the car too much, but they rarely tell you which color to use.

Most of the time, the colors used are dark blue, grey, or red, but other factors can make the color vary. Sometimes, the new car has not yet been brought out on the market, and there are no pictures on the Internet. All the agency provides is a few shots, and, believe me, they are usually not very useful because you have to reproduce shots that are different than the reference pictures.

It's a good idea to keep a couple of small models of cars in the studio and to practice drawing them from all different angles. Become familiar with the various views. It won't matter if the model is different than the car you are drawing for the board. You can figure out the details from the reference picture received from the agency.

Also, it's a good idea to have a few brochures of cars in your studio so you can study various details such as the shape of the headlights, the way the trunk of the car cuts in, the placement of the grill and the grill pattern, the lines of the car, and other features.

If the client is undecided and struggling with choosing a color, suggest the usage of black and white instead of colors. It may be difficult to convince the client of this, but it will save a lot of time in the long run. Adding a monochrome shade gives the board more value. You should have samples of this in your portfolio or on your website to help make the client's choice easier during meeting time.

Once, I created a storyboard for a finicky client and the agency wanted a very elaborate board. During the presentation, the client was distracted by all the details in the drawings and raised a lot of questions that delayed the progress of the meeting. The agency asked me to simplify the board, remove all details, and create a monochromatic color scale so there would be no obstacles in discussons with the client.

After a lot of experience, you will notice how similar that certain works are in structure. If you analyze a generic commercial you will see the different components:

- Intro
- Action
- Product Close-ups
- Reaction
- Packshot

Certain shots are inevitable, such as the product shot. Remember, you have to sell a product, as that is the purpose of the commercial. Considering that the average length of a commercial is about thirty seconds, you can easily see how routine the work can become. For example, you will automatically know and incorporate the fact that in each commercial the packshot or final product or logo should be visible for at least five or six seconds.

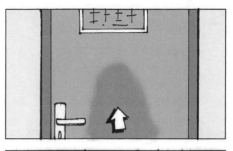

CRANE
UP

Ocean Spray
Cranberry
Classic

**Cleans your body
not your thoughts.**

Ocean Spray
Cranberry
Classic

The Pitch

Sometimes, an agency producer approaches the artist about a job, informing him or her that the job in question is really a pitch that is not yet approved by the client, just a proposal in which the agency is investing time and money, in hopes of hooking a client. Basically, what the producer wants is to limit the costs since it is not certain that the agency will get the job. What does this mean for the artist? In many cases, it means that the artist's fee may be reduced by up to half the usual rate.

It's all in the negotiations, though. Sometimes, you can agree on a fee and an additional payment if the job goes through. However, you should be aware that in most cases the job does not go through. Accepting pitch fees means that the agency is obligated to stay in contact with the artist and use him or her for the work if the job has been approved. It can be stressful to wait and wonder. On the other hand, because the artist is doing the agency a favor of sorts by working for a pitch fee, the pitch job can be easier than some other jobs as the artist may have a little more freedom in choosing what is best for the presentation, how much to produce, and whether to create a color or black-and-white board. The artist may even be able to drastically reduce the number of frames produced.

Just be aware when the job is a pitch job, so you won't be surprised when you send the invoice and the agency calls and asks, "We didn't get the job. Can you offer us a pitch fee of 50% of this invoice?" Of course, this is unfair to you. You should always know before you do the work whether it is a pitch job or not. If the agency doesn't tell you, ask about it before you invest your time.

The Animatic

At times, the agency is under pressure from the client to test a film commercial idea. In that case, the agency may need to screen the commercial for a target market audience. Enter the animatic, which is basically an animated storyboard. As animation goes, the result is not a polished piece, but more like a slide show with sound, dialogue, and music.

To produce it, the artist needs to draw more frames than usual and work on details, but also create continuity for the client that is much more generalized than what a director might prefer. In a way, the animatic is much more conventional and straightforward and less technical. For example, certain camera movements, such as crane shots and effects, are simply suggested rather than included. To create a proper animation would take considerably more time, and since budgets and schedules are always limited, the artist must remind the agency of the limitations.

The main tip I can give an artist for animatics is to work in layers. If the character should move her eyes in a close-up, you need to draw the eyes separately and then draw separate layers to create whatever else is needed. Do that and you will be able to produce the frames without hassles.

Other advice I can offer is to use the computer to add colors and save the original files so you can make adjustments and revisions without any problems. This will save you a lot of time.

Usually, the storyboard artist doesn't actually produce the animatic. That part of the job is typically done by the agency or a postproduction facility. Believe me, it is better that way. In addition to drawing the pictures, someone has to record the voice, edit sound, and do multiple retakes and versions. All of this is time-consuming for the artist; in addition, most agencies already have contacts in place that take care of that part of the job. It's important, however, to be in touch with the third party in order to know what kind of material to produce.

The first question the artist must ask is what resolution is required, and in what format the animatic will be created. The size and details of that sort will be given by the animatic editor. Usually the JPEG format is the easiest to handle because of its reduced size, but sometimes the best solution is to deliver the material in layers in Photoshop files so the editor can move the elements around and work with them separately.

Planning the storyboard for an animatic is a little bit like working with animation. Artists have to plan ahead for all the resources they will use. A rough sketch of the whole sequence is important and should be created under the direction of the art director so there won't be any misunderstandings and nothing will be omitted.

The artist should take notes indicating where eventual movement or elements in the frame will have to be animated, but the editor will save the files in sequential order so that once imported into the editing program, the sequence will be easy to follow. All the editing programs work basically the same way and have the same layout.

In the event of changes and revision or the addition of new frames, one shouldn't renumber the frames but add letters so that the new frame won't be revised. If a new scene is added between frame 3 and frame 4, for instance, all of the new files would be named 3A, 3B, 3C, and so on.

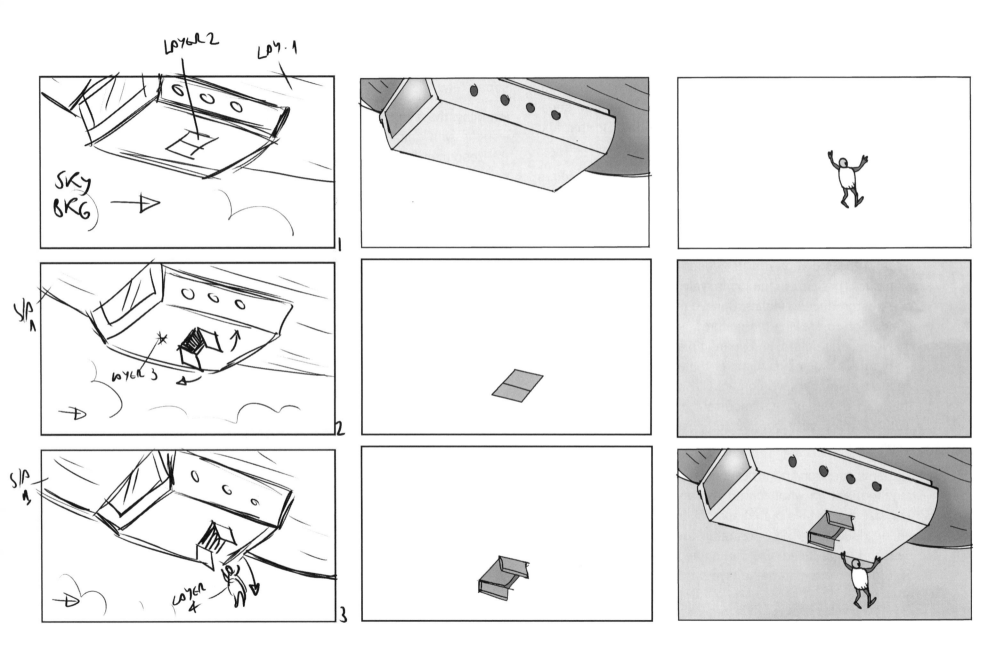

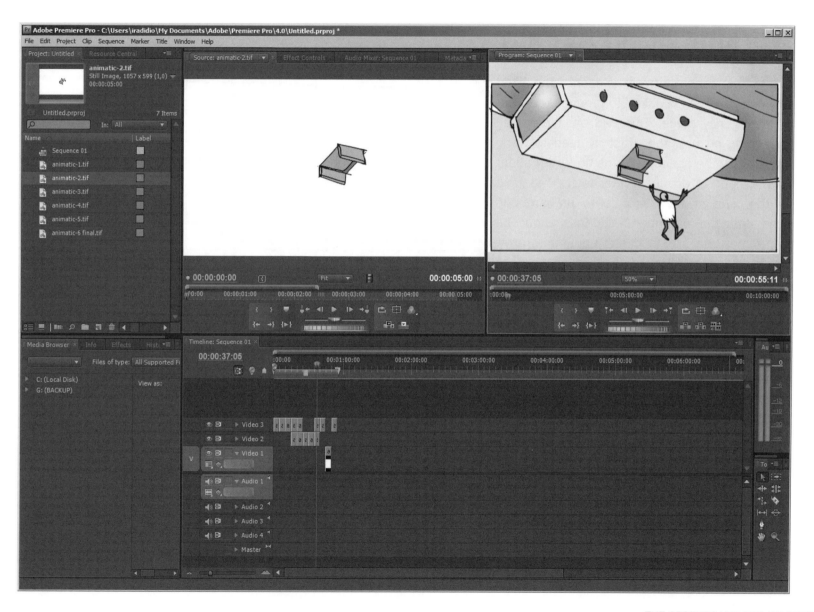

Working at an Agency

Due to time constraints at the agency, the artist may occasionally be asked to produce the work at the agency office. This can be a problem, depending on how the artist is used to working. Usually the agency informs the artist about such a need in advance, prior to the meeting, so that she or he has time to prepare and bring along the material needed for the job. But sometimes the artist doesn't know until arriving at the agency that the work must be done at the location. For that reason, I recommend having a few preprinted storyboard pages with the frames already planned. This will save a lot of time and help the work at the office go a lot faster.

At right are the preprinted frames I use regularly: the first two columns mostly for commercials, the third for feature films.

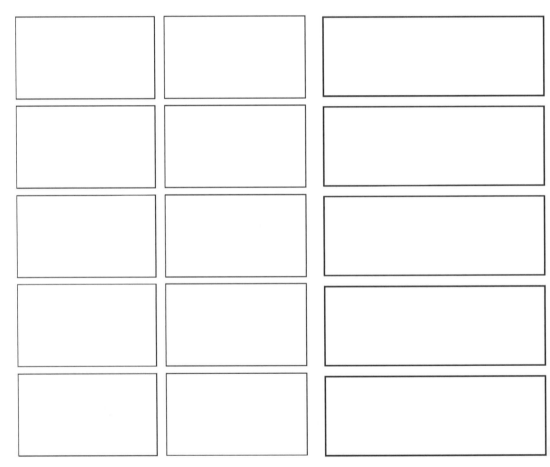

The agency may not have a light table, even though it is quite a common tool in advertising. If there is no light box, I recommend that you carry along a regular pencil and eraser. In fact, it can be effective to work the sketches with the pencil and later go over the pencil marks with ink.

Most likely, you will have to leave the original work since the agency will take care of the scanning and layout for the presentation. If that's the case, I recommend that you make copies of your work before you leave. In the event that the agency needs revisions or additional frames later on in the production stages, you will have copies to work with.

Similarly, make sure to take all of the markers and tools you normally use for your work. It's not guaranteed that you will have access to the things you need at the agency. Also, it's not professional for artists to show up without their tools.

I strongly suggest that when you work at the agency office, you do not show off, meaning that even if you are capable of producing the work in a very short time, you should take all of the time needed to work comfortably and smoothly. If you produce the work very quickly, you will be expected to work even more quickly the next time you work with the agency, which will push you. Your work could become sloppy if you are expected to work faster than you are comfortable with. Just stay within the deadline you have been given by the agency and you will be fine.

WORKING WITH DIRECTORS AND PRODUCTION COMPANIES

When the idea generated by the agency has been approved by the client, it moves to a production company chosen for the work. Invariably, the board will change in many ways because, even if the idea and the script are the same, the director's vision and the execution of the work or the approach are going to be different.

Occasionally, the same artist might be contacted to work for the production company, not because of the previous engagement with the advertising agency, but mostly by chance. Agencies rarely recommend the artist to the production company because they and the director may already have a list of artists they work with. However, a very active storyboard artist may have the chance to work on both assignments dealing with the same project. It won't change anything except that the artist already knows the project. In fact, the frames are hardly ever reused and a brand-new board will be produced from scratch.

The reason is that the needs of a production company are different than those of an agency; they are more concrete and technical. A production company needs to budget for the film, so the board is its tool to review the work, see how many shooting days they will need, how many scenes, and so forth. The board is also used by directors to see what needs to be added to the film in the matter of shots and style, to see if the idea works visually, to transfer their vision to the agency, and basically to indicate how they intend to shoot the film.

Some directors do a lot of homework, often drawing the board themselves. Some are pretty good at it, too. In those cases the communication with the artist is simple and direct. Many directors bring not only a great deal of reference material to the meetings, but also commercials, clips, images, and a detailed treatment, which is the first thing the advertising agency will actually receive from the production company. The storyboard is the next immediate step so that it can be presented to the client with all the necessary explanations. At this point, the storyboard becomes a shooting board.

Know Your Director

For many years, I have worked regularly with a few directors and employed methods and styles I have learned by doing job after job with them. We have established a good working relationship so that meeting prior to the job isn't necessary any longer. With just some basic notes regarding the treatment and script, I am able to produce the board they are looking for.

Even though jobs might be different for different products and targets, inevitably directors have a personal touch and style that can be recognized by people in the business. These directors create their own recognizable style by a particular choice of light, colors, framing, or narrative approach. Indeed, the work differs greatly from one person to another. But it's a good

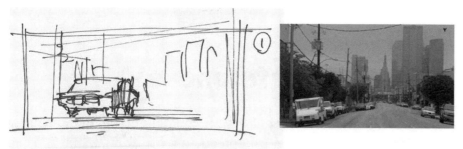

(1) New location. Car driving towards camera. Same location as traffic lights. Skyline in background.

I enjoy working with talented directors who can draw. Sometimes they give me precise instructions and their sketches are perfect guidelines for my work.

(3) Another angle of Kasey. Instead of being profile we're now in a 3/4 angle as he is driving down the street.

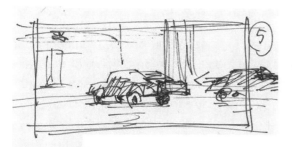

(5) New angle at the stop of traffic lights. Instead of being behind the cars we're now 3/4 of an angle behind.

idea for the artist to become familiar with various directors' work. It will benefit you when you attend meetings.

During the meetings it's common to talk about the reference material — films made by other directors, the work of a photographer, photographs that set the mood of the film — and these discussions offer hints indicating who the favored director may be. If that is the case, and you have worked with that director previously, this is the perfect opportunity to bring up references to that director and let the production company know that you have worked with him or her before. I also believe that a good storyboard artist should have a solid knowledge of filmmaking and the history of movies. Often cult and classic films, along with recent TV series, are used as references when discussing a project.

If you haven't had a chance to work with a director before, you can definitely check out his or her work on the Internet. Often, production companies display their directors' works on their website and it's good for you to view the work and start to understand it, as well as the production company's style and trademark. Production companies usually represent a number of directors and they always have a show reel available on their websites.

Use References

A good treatment always contains information about style and mood that the production company wants to achieve. At times the material provided to the artist is only what is available as a result of research. Details, such as the cast or the location, have not yet been defined. The information offered is just a vague inclination of what the company is aiming for, but in many cases the artist must later rework the board to include updated information.

The cast details are not terribly important in the beginning, unless the characters are drastically changed. Obviously, if the main character is changed to a man instead of a woman or a child instead of an adult, this affects the storyboard. Mostly the concerns with details come with the location, as you will need to have the right environment for the scene. For this purpose I suggest that, if the storyboard is otherwise accurate, you work with the storyboard draft until all locations have been chosen and finalized. Otherwise, you will waste an enormous amount of time and energy.

It might happen that, for meeting purposes, the agency needs a finished board, even though the information provided has not been finalized and approved. In that case, you should consider the job completed and ready for billing. In fact, any ulterior changes or the need for a new board constitutes a new job all together. Many agencies (when it comes to advertising), make it clear that the board will need to be updated in various stages as they go along with the development of the idea so the artist must have an appropriate agreement for the job.

If references provided to you are vague, as, say, in the instance that you are working for a clothing company that is not yet sure what product should be advertised (believe me, it happens all the time), there is no other way to do it than to produce a simple board, perhaps only focusing on key frames. The agency or the production company and the director will provide a mood board (an inspirational board to set the mood of the film), treatments, and other inspirational material such as photos and clips. Half of the artist's job is basically there, which results in copying the style and images that have been provided along with the script.

One of the reasons is that photos cannot be shown to the client because they are too clear and detailed and might mislead the client; for instance, if black and white photos are shown, the client might believe that the final film will be in black and white, even though the agency has pointed out that the photos are only for references. It also might look as if the agency hasn't worked much and, professionally, it isn't a good idea to show the work of someone else to explain a new idea for the campaign. In some cases, I have been asked to copy certain photos so the company could take the drawings to the meetings. It's as simple as that.

At other times, the photos included in the brief — usually, a PDF document that includes a treatment, script, casting pictures, location, and other information — are intended for brainstorming or to suggest an idea or a concept, and a storyboard artist should work from there. During the meeting, you should collect the material and get as many notes about the project as you can. An experienced artist will be able to grab from the references provided the essence of the film, especially when one knows the director's particular tastes and style. Along with the references provided, you should also ask for previous work produced for the same product or client so that you can stay consistent with the style and understand what kind of final result is expected. With the help of a good tablet, you can reproduce the photos given by the agency very quickly, but I suggest you find alternate images to copy when possible, so that you can leave a professional impression with the agency. For example, if a picture of the Tour Eiffel is provided, why not look for other images on the Internet so that you can change the angle or create a new composition?

Sometime the agency or the director gives precise instructions and the images provided serve only as a guideline for preparing a rough board, using images that can be traced later with the help of the light table or a digital drawing tablet.

Sometimes references are included in order to illustrate style or as an example of the photography or the color intended for the film.

109

Resources

I had planned to say that the Internet is the most important source of material for the storyboard artist, but recently my network connection died and I was without the Internet for almost a week, with the exception of my phone Internet for reading e-mail. At the same time, I had a few big jobs with tight deadlines stacking up on my desk. For some of the work, I needed to check out some online clips, download a few pictures, and so forth. It wasn't practical to do these tasks on my phone because of the small screen size and the expense of downloading images. (My mobile phone company would've been happy, but I wouldn't have been happy when I received the bill!)

I had to return to the old way of working with storyboard — the way I started back before the Internet was even conceived — using magazines and other reference material. I went to the library where I discovered that they had free Wi-Fi. Yes, of course there are the Internet cafes where one can work, but remember when I said that artists are lazy? Well, I had to draw a famous musician in a storyboard, so I got a music magazine that portrayed the musician in an interview. (I always keep an archive of material such as magazines, books, and brochures.) I also needed a picture of a car for another commercial, so I used my digital camera to take a picture. I had to draw a fish, a picture of which I found in an encyclopedia. By the end of the week, I had done all of the jobs on time. But I discovered that normally I wouldn't have encountered so much movement in my work. If I had had the Internet at my disposal, I would have just sat at my desk and worked for most of the week.

Seriously, one can find reference material just about everywhere. In general, every time I get a job assignment I ask the company to provide me with reference material. Most companies have already done the job of sorting out images, searching locations, and even finding reference clips. I can collect it all on my flash drive during the meeting, and I'm set.

If you are working on a long-term project, you can always invest some time in research. If you have connections within the film industry, for instance, you might have access to a prop warehouse, so why not get a friend to wear some of the costumes as a reference?

Other times, as I mentioned before, I use my digital camera or the one in my phone and get what I need on my way home from the meeting. Have you ever tried to draw the interior of a subway train or a bus from memory? There will be so many details you won't remember. You must get in the habit of gathering good reference material. It's part of the job of a good storyboard artist.

Improve Your Skills and Work Faster

It is a fact that the more you draw the better you become in both speed and composition. For that matter, I always encourage my students to carry a small notebook just to keep practicing and sketching whenever they feel inspired. You never know what will inspire you and give you the urge to draw something.

At the same time, discipline in practicing your art should be a commandment for an upcoming artist. Speed, as we now know, is one of the most important skills for a storyboard artist, and it so happens that a lot of directors much prefer sketchy work to well-inked and detailed illustrations that take the artist a long time to complete during a meeting. Recently I was working for a campaign and the director asked me to produce a few pictures of a model trying on outfits in front of a changing room mirror. Since I had a lot of time on my hands, I thought I would test a brand-new tablet I had

just bought and really got into it. I got so much into it that I spent the whole weekend working on the illustrations, adding shades, and using photos as references. But, in the end, when I sent off the material I received a comment from the director that he liked the pictures but he would much prefer if I did some really rough sketches. He said the work looked too polished for him to present at the meeting with the client. He wanted to present the idea in a more casual way because he had the idea of shooting the film with a handheld camera like a music video, while the illustrations suggested a larger-than-life set and different setup and style.

So I went back to my board and reproduced it quickly so as to match the director's needs. As it turned out, I could have simply finished the whole job in less than an hour and the director would have been happier if I had not gotten carried away. Lesson learned. There is a time to be inspired and get carried away, and there is a time to stick to what is needed for a particular job. It's best to know which time is which.

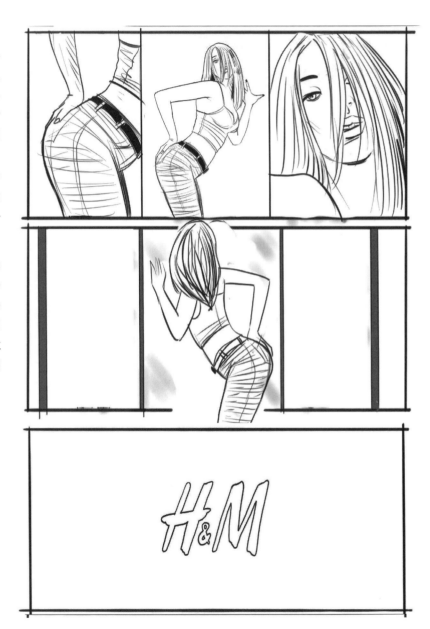

Speed is a skill that can only be improved by drawing a lot. When one has achieved a certain level of confidence, it will become natural to approach a board, sometimes with very little sketching. It happens that when I work on feature films, I produce the frames during the meeting and won't need to clean them up.

Drawing a car hundreds of times makes you capable of creating the picture with just a few strokes and lines. The same is true for creating characters and other objects. The best exercise is just to practice drawing at different angles, starting from a single image.

When it comes to the human body, remember the little notebook I suggested you always have in your bag. Nothing is better than sketching in public places from live scenes. Try sketching in a café or on a subway train. This way you can learn to be very efficient in your sketching because you only have a few moments to look at the scene and get it down on paper.

I used to visit bookstores frequently, as well as magazine and comic shops, because I could find interesting titles to add to my library. The illustrations in photography books serve as inspiration and as material useful for practicing composition.

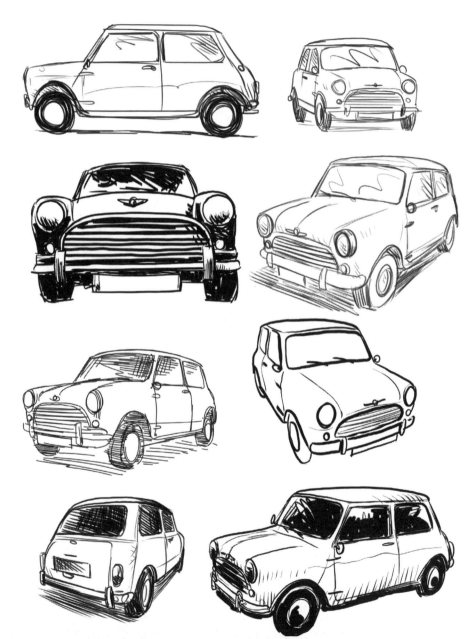

STORYBOARDING MOVIES

8

The movie industry comes right after the advertising agency as a possible source of work for the storyboard artist. In some cases, the connection to the movie industry happens in the advertising world because movie directors are hired to work on TV commercials. But it also happens that advertising directors move on into the feature film world and may want to take their favorite storyboard artists with them.

This is one of the reasons why it's important always to act professionally and build a network of contacts. Knowing who the director is and knowing his or her previous work can build up your confidence. Also, staying in touch with the producer of the job is very important since the producers often follow the directors into their personal projects.

There are various stages of production in the making of a film, and the storyboard artist's work might be required on different levels. During the preproduction phase, for example, when the producers are looking for funding or sometimes even before that when a scriptwriter or a director wants to sell a movie, the storyboard artist's work will be a little different than when the movie is being shot.

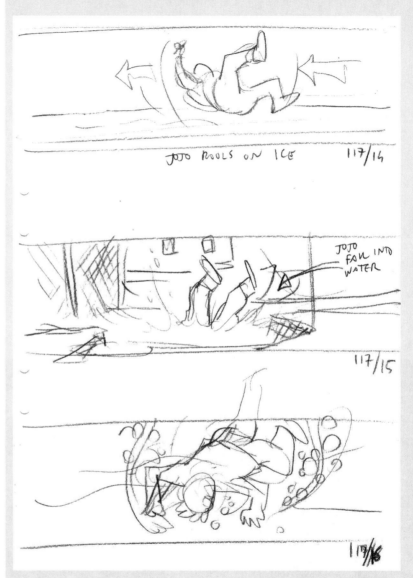

It's not unusual for a director to ask you to draw some pictures to provide inspiration for a project. Sometimes, during the scriptwriting phase, pictures can be useful in getting everyone into the mood of certain scenes.

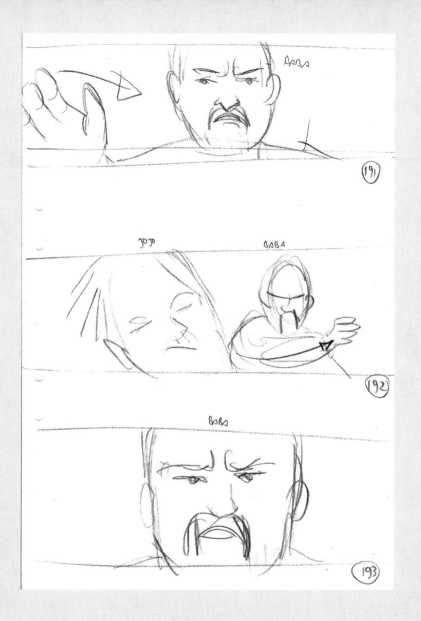

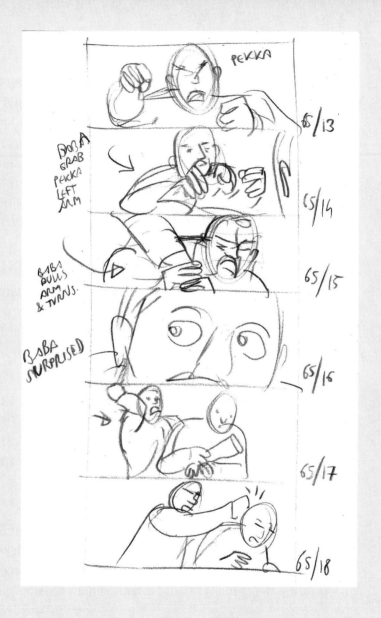

A director might have had a project waiting for a producer for years before meeting a storyboard artist to visualize his or her vision. In recent years, more and more producers have realized how important it is to present a film with an adequate storyboard, even if it is not exactly a shooting board. Things will eventually change once the project is given the green light, but, for the purpose of presentation, providing a series of well-crafted illustrations is always a good way to promote the movie to investors.

Here is a tip: Get in touch with scriptwriters, perhaps on their first attempt at selling a script. It is not common for a writer to present a storyboard with the script, but it could be useful for the writer if it attracted a producer. The storyboard is also valuable in helping the scriptwriter gain experience and become familiar with the feature film world.

Some directors may already have a precise idea of what they are looking for or already have a rough storyboard that they've created on their own and are looking for an artist to translate their scribbles and doodling for the rest of the crew and team.

As with script development, a storyboard can go through a lot of revisions before finally being shaped into a proper shooting board. Therefore, I suggest that you develop the quickest sketching style for the work-in-progress and for the long meetings with the director. Eventually, artists should consider finding an assistant to help out with polishing, inking, scanning, and organizing the work when schedules are tight.

It can be difficult to know who is in charge of a production, especially when the project has not yet been finalized. Additionally, it's not that simple to stay up to date with the industry unless one has connections on the inside.

My first advice is to contact the film institute to get the listing of the production companies that are active in the market. Then, with the help of the Internet, you can search their Web sites and contact the producers individually, asking for a meeting. Some of them might reply and will visit your Web site for more information about you, but when possible, I think a proper meeting is the best way to approach producers, especially if you have a wide range of styles and samples to show. An e-mail might be restrictive and could limit the possibilities; plus, during the meeting you might receive information about their current productions and get contacts with directors or other producers.

As I mentioned before, the storyboard can be used to scout for financiers, but also to get funding from the state or other organizations. And it might just happen that before the meeting with you, the producer hasn't thought about having a storyboard produced for that purpose.

At some point, many TV commercial directors decide to move to feature films. Often, they will start by producing short films, sometimes with the help of the production company for which they work or that represents them. This allows them to experiment and also to keep down expenses. Short films serve as displays at festivals, but also help directors gain credibility needed to work on larger projects, such as motion pictures, as well as enrich their portfolio. In some cases, short films are demo or test versions of the actual feature film they have wanted to do for a long time or simply a couple of scenes to suggest the look and mood of the film.

Analyzing Scripts

Until the shooting starts, scripts usually undergo various stages of revisions and updates, in some cases affecting much of the storyboarding process. Sometime the storyboard causes the changes, especially when the director realizes how a scene can be improved. I have worked on productions where each time I met the director he brought a new version of the script and we spent most of our meetings reorganizing the board and updating the sketches. That happened because we were working on a script that was still under development, but due to tight scheduling, the storyboard had to be started.

The first thing an artist should do, even prior to accepting the work, is read the script, not just the treatment. Often the production doesn't have a final approved draft, but it is better than reading a synopsis. At least you have a better idea of the resolution of the scenes, the dialogue, the action, and so forth.

From the script, you can definitely understand the tempo and get a feeling for the general mood of a movie, even if the director might have a completely different opinion about how things will be staged.

Remember that the technical description in the script is not going to be considered. What you should concentrate on is the essence of the film. Try to imagine the situation you are reading about and imagine the dialogue of the characters. Action

SC. 89

SC. 90

scenes are more about what happens than how they are orchestrated.

It might be difficult to know how much you should research for the storyboard. For example, if it is a period film, you must understand what the costumes and designs of the period look like, as well as have some knowledge of the time and place. In a way, it's like going back to school for a history class. Fortunately, modern technology means you don't have to spend days in a public library. Instead, you can access all the information you need on the Internet.

From the script the artist can estimate the efforts and the difficulty, as well as the amount of time it might take to execute the job. The artist can also get a feel for whether the story works. A friend of mine translates scripts, and sometimes he tells me how the script he is working on is missing something or has a weak plot. By the time he receives the scripts, they have already gone through a lot of changes and revisions and are supposed to be ready, but there is often still unfinished business. The same thing happens with the storyboard process.

From the number of pages of the script you can determine the approximate length of the movie. One script page equals about a minute of film. Dialogue, sometimes referred to as "talking heads," is nothing the storyboard artist should be concerned with. In fact, sometimes the director deals with the dialogue using a floor plan, a rough sketch of the location from above on which the director and DP mark camera positions and movements.

I mostly focus on transitions between scenes since those require a lot of time sketching and trying to resolve. Often writers escape the problem by just writing "Fade Out" at the end of each scene, so most of the artist's work entails "connecting" scenes with each other to create continuity.

Sometimes the work is difficult if the script is not very visual or the description is superficial. Another interesting, but rarely mentioned, problem is created with a dream sequence. All directors have their own opinion about how to visualize a nightmare or a dream sequence, but it is never well illustrated in the script. The same goes for flashbacks. If a script contains several dream sequences or flashbacks, the work can be a great challenge since in most cases you will have to use different styles and storytelling for the different parts of the script. It is not a simple matter of deciding that flashbacks are displayed in black and white while the rest of the film is in color. Narrative has become more sophisticated, and the flashbacks must be styled as a continuous part of the movie, as if the past is in the present.

As an example, a woman may be thinking of her past and the camera could pan over a window showing a scene from her past. A situation like this would be created during the meeting with the director and won't be found in the script. Another example would be if a character is telling a story to another character, and as they are sitting in a bar the camera pans around, bringing the story she is telling into focus or giving the impression of going back in time.

Here is a checklist you should consider when receiving a script, in order to estimate work and time:

- Time and place of the story
- Special effects/design
- The other productions the company has done
- The other movies the director has made
- Amount of work already done in preproduction
- Whether the cast is already in place
- Scheduled shooting
- Whether the script you have is the most current script

Organizing the Work

Storyboarding movies requires a great deal of discipline and organization. An entire feature film could amount to 1500 frames or more, and it is easy to lose track of them between meetings. One of the problems is that often the script is still in development when the storyboarding process begins, leading to revisions and adjustments of the boards. Often, the meetings are not highly organized and rescheduling happens frequently. Therefore, you can't really create a routine that works for everyone since there are so many people involved, from the production to the director to the various departments.

Sometimes, the storyboard work is devalued, especially by the people who are not directly dealing with it, such as producers, who may not comprehend the time really needed to produce a detailed board. I mentioned *detailed* because usually producers are the ones requesting details that are not really a priority for the work.

Directors are in control of the storyboard because, just as for artists, their work doesn't stop once the meeting has ended. Instead, they must do their homework, and this can result in extensive revisions after the meeting. For these and many other reasons, a professional artist must get and stay organized in order to prevent delays in delivery, avoid creative blocking, and prevent a nervous breakdown.

One of the artist's first organizational tasks is to make sure that the production company has provided him or her with all of the updated information, such as the latest script, shooting location, and casting.

Second, the artist must obtain direct contact information for the director and all of the people involved in the storyboarding process. You should remember to get phone numbers as well as e-mail addresses so you have multiple ways of contacting the person you need to speak with. Similarly, you should also leave your contact information with them. Handing out a business card with your mobile phone number and e-mail address to individuals is the best way to ensure you can be contacted with updates and changes.

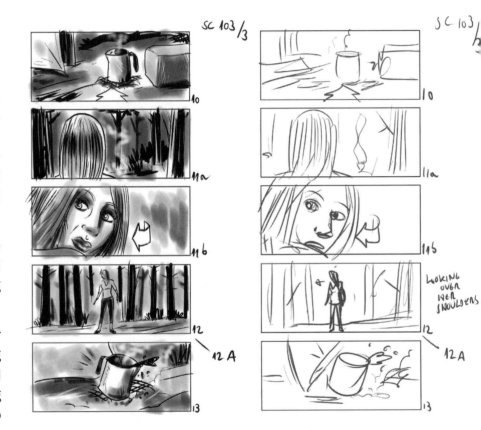

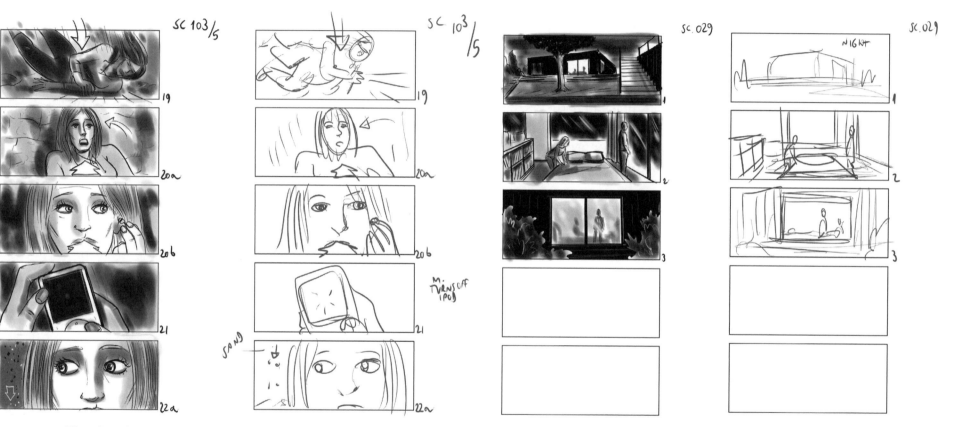

When I produce sketches for a feature film, I am careful to maintain the correct numbering (scene and take) so I do not confuse the production team because sometimes the team could start working using the preliminary sketches I have produced during the meeting to make their shooting plans.

It's important to discuss the method and execution of the work with the producer so there won't be any misunderstanding, and so they are well aware of what they are going to receive from you and when and how. For that purpose, samples of style and resolution should be shown during the very first meeting in order to establish how the final storyboard will look. In fact, also take samples of sketches and rough boards because many times the artist is required to produce a quick board and make changes at the last minute. This way, the production has an overview of all the possibilities and artist's abilities.

Be sure to negotiate an adequate fee for the job because many times, actually most of the time, there will be more work involved than you were initially told. Some artists prefer to negotiate a weekly payment so they can count on regular income and not have any delays in payment.

It's important not to burn bridges when working for a company. You never know when you may be called on to work for the company again. It's best to keep your options open and not let misunderstandings over payment prevent you from doing future work with the company. For this reason, you should be organized in providing quotes for the company and in your billing.

Once the job schedule is defined, purchase a few binders for that job, each of which should fulfill a specific purpose: one for the sketches, one for the reference materials, one for the finished work.

Artists should organize and store their storyboard by scenes. Frequently during a meeting the director is not ready to view the scenes in consecutive order and will want to skip some scenes until a future meeting date. For this reason, the artist should always read the entire script through at least one time. While reading, take notes regarding the characters and their roles so you can become familiar with them. Of course, the production company might give out the synopsis of the film, but it will lack important information that is necessary to delve into the story. The bottom line is: Be prepared for the work.

Some production companies prefer the storyboard to be delivered frame by frame, which is very labor-intensive, especially during the scanning process. Sometimes, they also want to receive the storyboard as soon as the artist produces the frames, which is also another time-killer because the artist's focus and concentration are broken by the distraction of the scanning.

I recommend designating a precise time for the scanning or maybe fit the scanning into a time when you are not focused on the project, so it doesn't distract you from the work. However, it's important to warn you against letting the scanning go for too long, piling up papers on your desk, and getting stressed about putting everything together at the last minute for delivery. That is not a good way of working and it might even waste more of your time since you might lose track of the work-in-progress.

Never promise what you can't deliver. You should take the time to evaluate the work before making estimates and setting a deadline. Always calculate more time than you actually need. For example, if you think that the work will take about six weeks, simply count two months for the execution of it.

Make sure those with whom you are working understand the procedures required, such as the meetings (very time-consuming), the cleaning up of the sketches, the scanning, and other tasks. Some people forget that the job of an artist begins once the meeting is over.

Dividing the job by scenes is a convenient solution for making eventual changes in the script. Sometimes scenes may need to be deleted or other ones added. If one works by scene, any insertion of new material is possible without having to renumber or reorganize the whole job. A good way to rename scenes is by their names, the way they are reported in the script, of course.

The artist should be concerned about the final organization of the storyboard because it will be the responsibility of the production company and whomever is appointed to file the board, add production notes, copy it for the team, and so forth. Usually, directors will also add notes to their copy of the board, just like everyone else. The artist should make it easy for everyone to access and understand the board progression.

Creating a website with client access can facilitate communication between the artist and the production company. The artist could simply upload the work-in-progress so that it can be downloaded by any member of the production team at any time. Again, the artist should be as accurate as possible with the material, deleting old files, especially when uploading revisions. Because it is easy for production people, especially

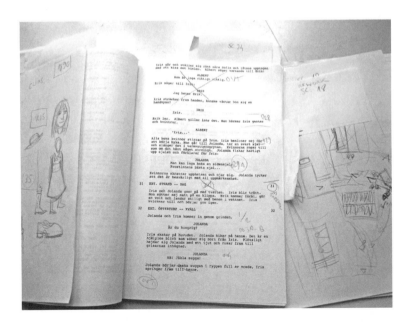

those not present during the storyboard meeting, to file the wrong material, it is better to avoid any misunderstanding by keeping only the current, updated material posted. This will also help the artist avoid wasting valuable time by sending outdated e-mail and attachments, courier-delivered files, and so forth. Keeping the files updated will streamline the whole process and save time for everyone.

I recommend that you produce storyboards by strips and not as singular frames. For one reason, the latter would require a huge number of images to scan, but on the other hand, the continuity of the frames might be messy using the strips method when additional frames are added during the execution of the job. Just make sure the numbering is always correct. Once the scene has been completed, you can reorder the frames progressively, still keeping the numbering, by using the cut-and-paste option in programs such as Photoshop. If new frames are necessary in the sequence already drawn, you can use a special numbering so that it won't affect the whole scene. For example, between frames 2 and 3, you can add 2A, 2B, 2C, and so forth.

Most important of all, artists should note on their copy of the scripts all the frames, references, and notes taken during meetings so that they are in full control of the work and know exactly where everything goes.

Write the number of the frame next to the dialogue lines.

The Meetings

Meeting the producer is a formality, not a necessity when the director has already decided on the style and the artist. The meeting with the producer is basically to decide the fee and to get an agreement, pure and simple. Most producers are not involved with the creative side of the movie but want to keep an eye on the expenses. The meeting with the producer will sometimes involve the director, but usually the negotiation does not concern directors.

Producers are not interested in many details, and bringing your references and explaining in general how the work will be made is more than enough for them, given that they will usually have very little time for meetings. Most likely, that meeting will be the only meeting with the producer until the production party months later.

Meeting directors is where the fun begins. The first time very little will be done from the script, as the director and the artist become familiar with each other and adjust to each other's work methods. The director will tell the artist his or her vision, the references to be used, the story conflict, the characters, and so forth.

The artist will show his or her portfolio, take notes, and ask questions. This is the time to bring up the notes taken during the read-through of the script. Also, this is when the

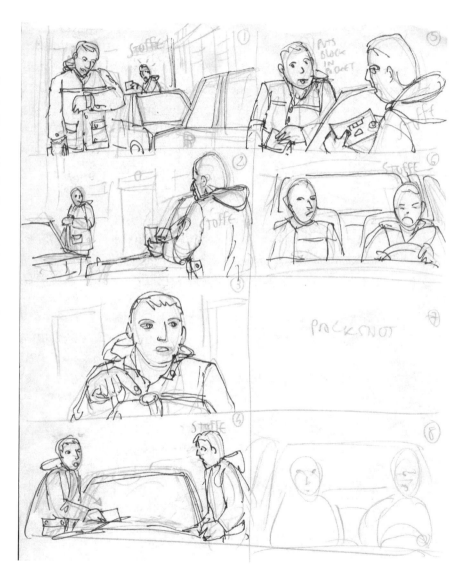

artist's knowledge of films, as mentioned before, is very important. The director might become quite technical when speaking about the movie, and he or she will expect the artist to be prepared and understand what is being said. The director may be stressed during the meeting and will not want to pause to answer technical questions for artists who haven't done their homework or who haven't gained a good knowledge of films. The artist must also be patient during the meeting, as other production members may ask questions concerning organization and such.

Don't be shocked if you arrive at the studio for your meeting and find that the meeting has been rescheduled for a later time in the day or for another day. It's best to take along some work to do while you wait so you don't lose focus on the job. My usual method of working with feature films is to make sketches during the meeting using a red pencil, and when the director is busy with other matters I continue with a pen to do a rough cleanup of the drawing. That way, once I am back in my studio and can use the light table, my work will go much more quickly.

A little tip I would like to offer is to try to get the meetings with the director to take place outside the production offices. Perhaps you can meet at your studio, or sometimes directors may prefer to meet at their place, which gives them a better and quieter environment. Working in a coffee shop can also help break up the office routine.

Sometimes the director will bring along the cinematographer. It's seldom that a storyboard artist would sit alone with the DP, but it may happen that the DP prefers to work on his or her own storyboard to establish the setting of the cameras and the shots needed to be taken. DPs need to know what lenses are required for each shot, and changing lenses can take some time; therefore, they schedule the shooting so that they can use the same lenses for as many shots as possible in a sequence. The DP's sketches are very useful because they show the exact position of the cameras and, in some cases, the studio produces miniatures of the set so that the director can better plan the shooting.

Other times, a stunt coordinator might be brought in during the meeting. This is a very practical way to work on special action sequences. The stunt coordinator always has a clear idea of what the scene would be, and his or her job is to make seemingly impossible things happen very naturally. They have all the answers and solutions. It is quite entertaining as well, since stunt people tend to be quite visual in their performance. At times, the artist will work with models and toys. For example, little toy cars can be used to plan a chase scene or an accident. Fights and special action scenes will also be rehearsed, and it can be useful to observe some of those; ask if you can take pictures with your digital camera.

Many times, when feasible and appropriate to do so, the director might want to take the artist on location to see the actual place where the shooting will take place. That provides another opportunity to use your digital camera to take pictures that you can use as reference material.

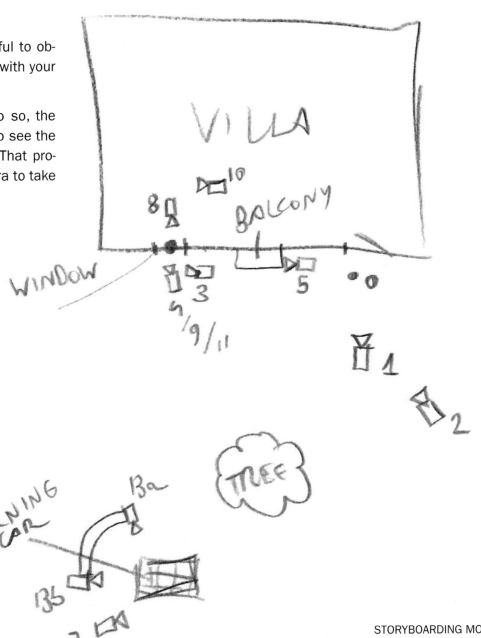

The Conceptual Artist

On occasion, it happens that the artist is asked to produce other kinds of work for a production, such as design or concept art. In some cases, even before the storyboard process begins, the production company needs to approach investors, but they do not have a final draft of the script. In that case, the storyboard artist needs to produce key frames or art that is mainly used to attract producers.

Conceptual art assignments can be a hassle if the production companies are not used to working that way. In fact, the company representatives might not know what to expect or what to ask you for. They might bring up examples of paintings to describe their needs, but since they know very little about the execution of the job, the paintings might not be sufficient. The artist can help by taking a couple of reference books on the making of films to the meeting. The how-to film books usually contain a variety of production art produced for the films, as well as storyboard panels that show what a conceptual drawing looks like. Chances are that most of them have never seen any of these drawings and will find them very helpful.

Once, I was called by an upcoming production company for a feature film, and I was asked to produce ten conceptual illustrations that were supposed to be used to secure funding from the film institute and other sponsors. I later learned that they had also planned to use the pictures to accompany the script they intended to send to the desired actors' agents.

They had a dream cast in mind but weren't sure about the availability of the actresses they wanted. Initially, the story was about a group of elderly ladies involved in a big adventure, and they made it clear that the women should look like anyone's grandmother. I executed the sketches, and after I received approval, I completed the pictures. But I knew already that I would have troubles.

The dream cast they had in mind included some big names, and they weren't exactly grandmothers. I couldn't draw them because it wouldn't have made sense for the script, so I kept them anonymous and proceeded to draw happy grandmothers. Of course, the producer was not happy with the results and asked me to draw the dream cast but to make them look older. I didn't object, even though I knew the drawings would not appeal to the actresses. I drew them older and the comments came right after bringing back the anonymous grandmothers but with fewer wrinkles. Ultimately, the film didn't go into production and I am sure that the producer is still blaming the illustrations.

When working on conceptual art, expect to have to make a lot of revisions and changes, and even to start all over a few times. Patience is a great virtue for a professional artist. In order to avoid frustration, it's a good practice to store all the e-mail communications and, of course, all the production sketches in an archive so you can double-check any time there are misunderstandings or communication issues.

If working with the computer, it is good always to keep the work-in-progress files and rename them after each revision, using the current date of the changes so that the previous file is still recoverable.

Always be completely sure about approvals before adding colors to an illustration. Your quote needs to be accurate, while at the same time covering everything that you need to do for the storyboard. Every additional task means you will be using more of your valuable time, and your time must be compensated for. Don't assume anything — try to get as many specific answers as you can when providing a quote or a time frame for a job.

I assure you that the production company doesn't usually know and understand the time needed for execution. Always allow yourself plenty of time to get the work done so you won't be terribly stressed about delivering the project on time. There will be enough stress toward the end of the project without having to worry that you won't finish on time.

I don't want to make it sound as though storyboarding is a terrible job. I promise: It is a lot of fun working with conceptual art because more time is given to the artist to execute the work, and there is much more artistic freedom. But the best part of the job is that this work might be published in the before-mentioned how-to art books or at least shown in the special features of DVDs. Sometimes the concept art is even used to promote the film in magazines and such.

Watching Movies with a Different Eye

Well, there is one thing that you will hate about the story-boarding profession — the fact that it will be much easier for you to spot mistakes in movies. Not only that, but you will also start to notice subtle hints and foreshadowing in the film, and this will ruin the whole surprise of the movie for you. Inevitably, you will start watching movies in a different way, the professional way. It is only natural that certain details will catch your eye. I used to watch movies with a friend, a scriptwriter, and while I was anticipating the next scene, he would say the dialogue lines out loud before the actors said them.

CONTRACTS AND LEGAL MATTERS

Without fail, when it comes to long-term assignments the artist should make sure there is a proper contract or agreement. This is especially important when working on movies. Chances are higher that the project might be delayed or canceled, and to avoid nonpayment for work that you've spent a considerable amount of time on, you must ensure that your contract includes a kill fee of 50% that is paid at the signing of the contract. This way, at the very least you will be paid half of what is owed if the project dies.

Do not work on verbal promises because in the movie industry production people come and go, and by the end of the movie, chances are that the contact with whom you made a verbal agreement may be gone. Besides that, working for a movie can mean that you attend many meetings and create a large number of frames, which will engage your time for a couple of months or more. You don't want to have to wait such a long time before collecting some of your fee. You have to pay your bills and provide a living for yourself during the months that you are working on the storyboard.

Another good reason to insist on a contract in writing and advance payments or weekly payments is that at times the artist might be working with a colleague or will need the assistance of other persons who would be very disappointed if things didn't go as expected and they weren't paid on time.

Contracts don't need to be complicated. The most important factors of the contract include a specified deadline or schedule. Since the number of frames required for the entire project can't be accurately estimated, you should refer to the work as "the entire board," even though many scenes won't require elaborate boards, such as those for "talking heads."

The beauty of storyboarding movies is that each time it is a completely different challenge and environment. Each studio has its own way of approaching the storyboard process, and, depending on the preproduction or the phase of the production, things can move forward at a different pace. The worst scenario is when the production is late and everything needs to be speeded up, but that's another story.

Artists need to know who is in charge and not rely solely on the director who might have contacted them. In fact, directors are not very aware of the budgeting and, in some cases, might not have consulted with the producer before calling their favorite artist on board. So it is in your best interest to get to know the producer also.

First the artist will have to read the script and know what the job involves. Then, the artist should meet the producer or whoever will be in charge of the contract. In between, the artist should investigate the production company and its team to find out what projects they have worked on before. This will help the artist understand the volume of work expected for the current project. It also provides the artist with the security of knowing that the company is active in the market.

Before signing the contract, the artist should finally evaluate the work, determine what kind of commitment is required to meet the suggested deadline, and to consider all matters to avoid the risk of taking on an impossible task.

Big production companies already have a template for artist contracts and in most cases the conditions are fair. Just make sure that you have read it thoroughly before signing. I know many artists who still don't think it is important to know what one is signing. Sometimes they learn the hard way.

In the advertising world, in general, there are no contracts, since all the jobs are done by the end of the day for the next day. Occasionally, the artist will be asked to sign a confidentiality agreement when sensitive material or internal company presentations are exposed. The agreement is usually a simple form produced by the client. It's no big deal.

When it comes to the animation field, the artist is usually hired for a defined period of time, usually for the duration of the project or sometimes for long-term collaboration.

I always recommend that the freelancer artist keep a "window open" in the profession, even if a contract has been offered. You should always consider that you may be invited to give classes at an art school or do a storyboard for a commercial on the side. If bound by a contract, the artist may not be allowed to work with other production companies, especially if in the same line of work. So you can see that sometimes it's best for the artist to be hired as in independent contractor or freelancer instead of as an employee for the production company. Being hired as a freelancer means that the you will be responsible for your own taxes, but the advantage is that you are free to work on personal projects as long as they don't interfere with the work for the production company.

During production, there are many short periods of time when the artist is not busy because one phase of the production has been completed and the next one has not yet started. It would be a pity to have to sit at a desk and twiddle your thumbs during the down times. Artists who are not under contract can take on small side jobs or work on their own projects during short periods of inactivity.

For feature film production, it's a different story. The job assignment might run for one or two months. The artist gets offered a work-for-hire contract or a contract for the project. It is always negotiable, both the terms and the compensation, and for the most part the artist will be working in his or her own space and studio except for meetings and brainstorming sessions with directors at other studio facilities.

To reiterate: Before you sign any contract, it's important to read it and know what you are signing. Remember to insert a kill fee. As you continue to work in the industry, you will become more familiar with the contractual terms and will see that most of the contracts are similar to one another, even though each company may have its own contract. If you don't understand something, ask about it, rather than simply signing what you don't know you are agreeing to. Contracts are binding agreements. Whatever you agree to and sign is what you are legally bound to. Make sure your contract covers whatever legal jurisdiction you are working in.

Don't look at a contract as your enemy. A contract can be beneficial to you in the event that the company you are working for decides not to pay you or otherwise to create problems for you.

THE PROFESSIONAL STORYBOARD ARTIST

The thing that distinguishes successful professional storyboard artists from others is the way they present themselves and the impression they project to a potential or existing client.

One of the most important factors regarding professionalism is the reliability of the artist. This is top priority over everything else. Storyboard artists must establish reliability if they want to continue to work in their industry. If an artist is not reliable, he or she will be replaced and will not have the references needed to continue to acquire jobs.

When I started working as a storyboard professional, I didn't have many connections in the market like some do when they start their career. Suddenly, out of the blue, after having spent weeks of sending my portfolio to agencies, I received a call from a production company that was in desperate need of an artist to complete a job started by an artist who had suddenly disappeared and could not be reached. The artist went away on vacation before the job was completed. I later learned that the agency wasn't really happy with the artist's work for a number of other reasons also, but didn't know of any other artists. It happened that the samples I had sent the agency ended up on the right desk at just the right time. I managed to take over the job and did my best to complete it within the already tight deadline. After that, I think I became the agency's favorite artist.

Professional Organization

A reliable professional artist should always be available and efficient in any situation. For example, not long ago I was traveling for leisure and a job came available during my trip. It was really the continuation of a job that I had started earlier, and the agency was desperate to have some pictures updated as well as receive new pictures for its presentation with the client. I couldn't say no to the request, even though I was on vacation, because I had a good relationship with the art director and I wanted to keep that relationship. Furthermore, the agency needed the same style of pictures as I had previously produced. For the agency to change artists would mean changing styles, and it couldn't really do that without it being a time-intensive and costly process.

Except for my laptop, a block, some pens, and a little pocket notebook, I didn't have any of my usual equipment with me. I always carry a block and a few pens for any occasion that might arise, but also because I like to draw in my free time and believe that it is good practice for artists to keep a little notebook in their pocket.

The first thing I did was investigate the possibilities for being able to complete the job. I went to the reception desk at the hotel and asked if there was a scanner I could use. Now that would have been the greatest solution, but of course there was no scanner available. I then asked what facilities were in the proximity of the hotel, such as an Internet café and such, and the clerk pointed one out that was not really close at all. For a quick job on the fly, it wouldn't have been a problem, but I knew with this job there would be several e-mail exchanges with the agency and I would be sending images back and forth, so going the distance to the place the hotel recommended would not be feasible. The time difference between my location and the agency's was also a factor, as it was nine hours, and meant that I would need to communicate with the team during its business hours when the facility where I was would be closed.

I made rough sketches which I photographed with my mobile phone and sent to the art director for approval. That was the fastest way to get started, but I knew I had to resolve the scanner problem. I realized that I could purchase a small scanner for the job, since scanners are fairly inexpensive. I found the perfect one that I could connect to my laptop via USB, and everything went smoother from then on. For a couple of days my hotel room turned into a small studio, but I could use the time difference to produce the work without additional stress and I could still enjoy my vacation.

Efficiency, in fact, is one more skill an artist should master. Now, with the story above, I might have scared some of you, making you think that you could never take any time away for a vacation if you are a professional storyboard artist.

The thing is that you can manage to take time away when needed, but with this job, as with any other freelance job, you need to be always prepared for the phone to ring or an e-mail to come in with a request for you to do a job, and you will want to do your best to follow through and complete the job. I'll be honest with you: There will be times when the assignments may not be as plentiful as you would like them to be; therefore, if at all possible, you should take advantage of assignments when they are offered. This may mean working weekends and even some holidays when you don't want to and rearranging your schedule to fit in extra work at times. I know artists who could not cope with this type of working arrangement and they switched fields because of it. If you love your job and want to continue in the profession, you will have to make some concessions regarding scheduling of work.

Learn to take advantage of the slow periods when work is not coming in. Spend time drawing boards so you can leverage your experience into other jobs. Do the fun things that you enjoy doing while you have down time. Travel, work on hobbies, visit with family and friends, and make the time count. Then when a job comes in, you will feel like settling in to work again.

Organization means having an efficient working space, but also a flexible agenda. And, as I mentioned before, thinking ahead is always a good start. For instance, going on vacation with a block and pens in your suitcase is always an advantage in case a call comes in. You should also be prepared to work in just about any place. Be flexible and turn whatever space you have into your studio. If I listed all of the places I have done my job, it would take an entire chapter in this book! Everywhere is a possible studio when your main tools are simply pen and paper.

A digital drawing pad is also a good solution if you travel often. If you are a skilled artist, the pad will eliminate the need for a scanner. The pads are small and easy to carry around. The newest models offer versatility, so with the appropriate software you can produce excellent work that is already digitalized and ready to be e-mailed.

Your Studio

Your studio is the place where you are going to spend most of your time, so one thing is for sure — it must be a comfortable place. It has to have both natural light from a large window and good lamps, since many times you will find yourself working evenings and nights.

You really only need minimal furnishings in your studio, but you do need a desk. The desk should be wide, and, if possible, you should have a separate desk for your computer in order to separate office and working studio area. Your office is where you have your papers, invoices, contacts, phone, computer, and scanner, whereas your studio is where you draw, have your light table, reference books, and supplies. It is the same space but with separate areas for separate functions, and it is important that you keep things on different desks so that one action won't disturb the other. For example, if you are doing your tax declarations at your office desk, it may take days to complete, and you will need to leave your papers out on your office desk while you keep working on your boards or illustrations at a table or desk in another area of your studio at the same time.

I am telling you all of this because I know how very little patience many artists have, and I have been there myself. Certain things are not compatible, and something as simple

Contrary to the popular vision of a freelance storyboard artist's studio being messy and disorganized, I am a person who likes things to be quite neat and orderly. I like to have control over my space. Some of my colleagues have disorganized, chaotic studios, and they often complain about having too little time to do their jobs and no time to pay attention to the condition of their studio. I admit that I sometimes get a little messy and don't always maintain perfect order when I'm working, but you can't see this in my studio. It is well hidden!

as a bill on your desktop may be in the way and result in an interruption of a job. Stacks of office papers that you know you must eventually work through can be a terrible distraction for your creative side. It is best to keep your office separate from your studio work area, even though they are in the same room.

The studio space is where you basically draw. You will need to have all the pens and tools within reach, as there is nothing more annoying as when a pen suddenly runs out of ink and you don't have a replacement immediately available. For that reason, it's important to take the time to check your stock periodically and keep a list of the things you need to replace or stock up on. I also recommend that you visit your local art supply store on a regular basis. There may be a sale on the items you need. Buying supplies on sale or at discounted rates can stretch your supply budget and decrease your cost per job.

A professional artist might be working on several projects at the same time, so it would be good to have binders to keep the work-in-progress with all the references for that job on the desk or nearby for easy access.

One tip to keep up with schedules and various projects is to have a cork board over your desk where you can pin notes or put sticky notes of the to-do tasks as well as reference pictures or anything else that you need to look at constantly.

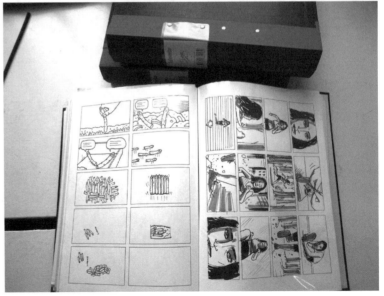

One typical problem many artists do not consider when setting up their working space is that the scanner has to be close to the computer, and really easy and quick to operate. Basically, there should be no effort required in using it since a good deal of the storyboard artist's work is to scan the job and finish it up on the computer.

Another issue that should be considered is that since the artist uses the Internet to look up reference images, the computer monitor should be well visible from the working desk. Of course, one can always rely on portable laptop computers for that function, if needed. Remember that these days all the material provided for the work (references, location pictures, PDF presentation, scripts) are usually digital, and the computer has a huge role in the work of a storyboard artist.

It might get messy! Yes, indeed, if you are working long hours, several days in a row on several projects at the same time, your plan for keeping your studio neat might be sabotaged. Therefore, the ideal solution is to outfit a completely separate room as a studio instead of using your living area. If your studio is a dedicated room, you can close the door and walk away from the work and the mess when you need to, without it affecting the rest of your home. You can eat meals without having your work on the dining table and relax without seeing your work.

An entire room might be a luxury for some, particularly if you have a family and have absolutely no extra place in your apartment. In that case, I recommend that you rent a studio.

Perhaps you can share the studio space with another artist or freelance professional so you can also share the rent to lower your cost. Another option may be to rent a desk in an office space. You can find ads for such arrangements at art supply stores, in newspapers, or on bulletin boards at art schools. This solution is usually quite affordable, but in some cases it might mean the artist would need to take on a part-time routine job to pay for the studio. This can be a problem for the artist who already feels strapped for time.

Bookkeeping

Here comes the painful side of things. Artists are not really good with bookkeeping, at least not the majority of them. For creative artists, the absolute numbers side isn't appealing. The fact that you have chosen this profession instead of a more traditional occupation might give you a hint that you are not a numbers person. The truth is that a creative mind often prefers not to be bothered with mundane issues and needs such as paying bills or doing taxes or sending out invoices. But, alas, these things are part of the business of storyboarding, and they must be done.

In general, keeping records is not a lot of work, but you do need to be organized sufficiently to list your expenses, save your receipts, keep track of your income, and have a good invoicing system in place. If you are not good with accounting for tax purposes, I recommend that you hire an accountant for tax-related tasks. The accountant will know how you should set up your records and how to help you save money with the deductible supplies and equipment you buy for your work.

Basically, the freelance storyboard artist should understand how to keep a history of purchases and the amount paid, as well as all business expenses such as telephone bills, studio rent, business travel fares, and other work-related expenses. I recommend setting up a simple system using binders for each part of the record-keeping system. For example, use one binder with a simple ledger sheet to record all expenses and purchases and the date of purchase or expense, and to save dated receipts in the order they are received.

At the same time, you can compile the data in an Excel document so that you can easily calculate and record the totals for each month. It is always a good idea to keep track of how much money you are bringing in and how much you are spending in your business.

Use another binder for invoices. Put the invoices in the binder in progressive order with a date and reference number. Again, you can also record the invoice information using accounting software that will keep running totals for you or simply use a ledger sheet. Knowing what invoices are outstanding at the end of the month will help you schedule the flow of work for the following month, and will let you know how much you are collecting from any one source or whether you should look for some new sources for work.

MONTH / YEAR

NR.	DATE	AGENCY	JOB	CONTACT	AMOUNT	SENT	PAID

When it is time for your accountant to do your taxes, you can simply hand over the binders if you have kept them updated; it will make his or her job much easier and save you money on the accountant's bill.

It sounds like record keeping is a really boring and tedious job, but if you keep the receipt when you make purchases and record when you pay bills, and note the invoice every time you send one, I promise this won't really steal much of your time. The worst thing you can do is put it off all year long and then try to remember everything at the last minute. Keep your records as you go, and when it comes tax time — you're all set without any headaches. Your accountant will love you for it!

Promotion

You have become an excellent artist and it is now that the fun begins. Promoting your work can be a profession on its own. In a way, you have to transform yourself into an agent and promoter, coming up with ideas to make your art visible and to be recognized in the market.

Of course, you have a website and your own network of contacts, but it's unlikely that people will find your website if they don't already know that you exist. The advantage of the Internet is that it's easier and much less expensive to promote a business or look up a service or business, but there is severe competition. Before, freelancers literally had to knock on doors and ask for a meeting to show their portfolio, but now they must find a way to direct potential clients to their website and look at the work online or request a meeting. So a big part of your job as a freelance professional is to have an online presence and market your service online.

Because I mentioned a portfolio, perhaps we could begin by looking at this subject first. In fact, what is more important than anything else is your work. When designing their websites, many artists spend a lot of time and effort in the design of the site, the text, and so forth. But really, what prospective clients want to see is samples of the work, and that should be the core of the site.

On the other hand, it's important to remember that an artist shouldn't count only on the Web to get work. Keep in mind that many publishers, agencies, and production companies still want to meet the artist in person, especially for promising long-term collaborations or a long-term contract. For that reason, it's necessary for artists to have a varied and organized portfolio to show work for the various fields they work in. It could be confusing for prospective clients if an artist is capable of working on many different styles and the clients don't understand which style best suits their particular project. Also, clients who need a rough board might view a sample of elaborate art in your online portfolio and think they should receive that elaborate type of work for the price of a rough board.

Depending on your abilities, interests, and fields, you should build up a collection of artwork for each target audience. Why limit yourself? Here are some general guidelines for a typical portfolio and what should be in it.

- **Size:** You should choose a size that is the easiest to transport and show around. This probably means that you will choose a standard 8½" x 11" size. This size is also standard for photocopying and will fit in any bag.

- **Advertising agency:** Include different kinds of boards — a large variety from a sketched board to an inked one — and color samples. In addition, include sample illustrations for posters and event designs. Don't include too many pieces of work, but include what is essential to show a variety of styles and resolutions that you can produce. You will have to act as a salesperson, and each of your samples will represent a certain price and time frame for completion. This will give the client a much better idea of what you can do than just telling them would do.

- **Movie or gaming industry**: If you are aiming for the movie or gaming industry, you should have a whole different portfolio. To begin with, the sizes of the frames are different. Sometimes each photocopied page will be one frame, but often the artist is commissioned to produce conceptual art and design, and eventually most of the work is produced on the computer. Again, you should display the various stages of production. It is my personal opinion that you should include a few samples of sketched boards. This will show clients how you proceed when you work directly with a director and what they can expect during meetings. Also, it will show your dedication and the stages necessary to accomplish the final board. This is useful, especially when discussing contracts. As I mentioned before, most conceptual artists use computer software to aid in their storyboarding, sometimes using 3D programs to accomplish the work. In that case, there is nothing else to do but add printouts to the portfolio folder. I would recommend that you also include printed flyers or a few samples that can be left on the meeting desk. It will give your prospective client a good impression.

If you have done quite a large amount of work, you might want to consider printing a booklet or small catalogue of your work to hand out to the people you meet. It is a good investment and it will be paid for by your first job.

A completely different task is building up an animation portfolio. In this particular case, you will need a little experience in the field. On the other hand, you have to begin somewhere, and you can start with showing that your skills in sequential art, movement, and drawing figures and characters are solid.

This particular field requires the artist to live in the studio, and production companies usually offer contracts for the entire time of production. This means that they have to select the right candidate carefully, since a storyboard artist has a lot of responsibility and should be working very closely with the director. Communication skills sometime are a plus in that case.

In addition to samples of storyboards, you should also include some character design, illustrations and poses, sketches of sequences, and samples of the storyboard using different techniques in an animation portfolio. For example, show work that was produced with markers, pencil, color, and gray tones to convince the production company that you are versatile, a useful quality in the field of animation. Consider that many of the jokes you see in a cartoon often are created during the storyboard process.

As for the website, you are free to choose whatever you want. I suggest that the design of the website be as simple as possible. Forget about all of the fancy animation and music that could potentially annoy the visitor. Avoid the long introduction that could bore and tire the viewer. Don't use a complicated menu that makes it difficult for anyone to navigate your site. If people have difficulty finding what they need on your site, they will quickly leave it. Simply, the only pages you need on your website are: Information, Galleries, and Contact. And that's that!

Many artists have blogs, which is a good idea. The blog can be incorporated into the website as a link, but don't use a blog for your main site. Your blog will probably not have the capacity for your sample images. Also, you don't know if you'll have the time and patience to keep the blog going and add new content to it constantly. The navigation of a

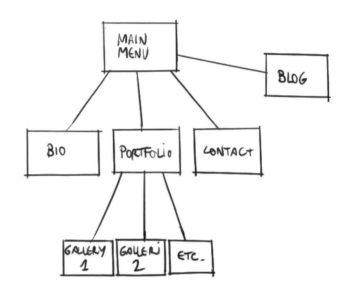

blog can be annoying, and blogs are not considered to be as professional as a website. Visitors sometimes deem blogs as "freebies" and may illogically associate the free blog with the value of the artist's work and deem it amateurish.

All you need to begin is a very good and easy-to-remember domain name and a simple menu. Your work will do the rest. Don't use long descriptions for your pictures. Let the pictures speak for themselves, with only pertinent information posted. Make sure you don't create confusion by putting too much stuff and information on the site. You can list a few testimonies written by satisfied clients. If you are just starting out and have no testimonials yet, do not write anything except your contact information and skills, which includes the material you

StoryboardAgency since 1999 has been producing works for animation, advertising, feature films and multimedia productions. Operating in Europe and USA we can be contacted 24/7, and for long terms project the work in progress can be monitored and downloaded from our password protected web site. Contact us for any further information.

Giuseppe Cristiano
Founder of Iradidio and the Storyboard Agency, he has been working in Europe and USA for over a decade, mainly freelancing for film production companies and the most known advertising agencies, with experience spanning from animation to feature film. He started up as a comic artist, for a few years he has been writing and drawing for a number of european publishers.

Marco Letizia
Comic artist from the start, has occasionally worked as illustrator. He has joined Iradidio being the second half of the Storyboard Agency. Since then he has been freelancing for the top advertising agencies in Europe and most recently he has been involved in films development. As well as drawing storyboards Marco produces illustrations for books.

Click on the names to see IMDB references

Web Design: Marco Letizia

By the way, if you are contacting a production company for a job, do not send an attachment. E-mail including an attachment might end up in the company's spam folder and no one may ever see it or respond to it. It is better to introduce yourself first and then ask if you may send some samples by e-mail. Then the company will recognize your e-mail and not delete it. But having a link to your website should be enough; if interested, potential clients will look up your work.

Another good practice is to be active during your spare time. This is a good time to do a local exhibit. It is easy to organize an exhibit at a local popular coffee bar or a bookstore in your town. The exhibit is always a good excuse to get in touch with companies or introduce yourself to new companies by sending them an invitation to the event.

Good professional artists are the ones who always look for possibilities in every situation and always have new ideas for promoting their work. Professional artists will keep their eyes and ears open and take advantage of what is happening in their area. If a festival is coming to town, why not get in touch with the organizers and offer to do illustrations for their posters or catalogues?

Several printers offer the print on demand option, which allows you to print only the number you need of anything, from a small catalogue to a complete printed book. Visit local printers and ask for their pricing sheet. You might find it easier and cheaper than you think to print out your own give-away portfolio.

At one point I produced a mock-up magazine of my work to use as a portfolio. The magazine is professionally done and properly published like any other magazine. The response to the magazine has always been good. Even today, people find my magazine on the shelves of various studios and contact me for work. I used to produce a different promotional item each year or so, such as a calendar, a small booklet, limited print illustrations, etc. It is always good to freshen up your professional image.

Very recently, I realized that social networks can be useful for promoting my work. In fact, for some of my latest exhibits, I used the social network platform to send invitations.

Freelance Survival Tips

I would say, when you work as a freelancer your look is as important as your work. You don't have to be an actor to get the job, but sometimes you give a first impression by the way you walk into a room. Self-confidence is important in this business, as it is in most other freelance professions. This means that you should walk toward your client with your head and shoulders up and extend your hand for a friendly handshake.

You don't have to have a style makeover, but when visiting an advertising agent or other company to talk about work, you should look somewhat professional. In different areas, there will be differences in what is counted as professional attire. The likes of Johnny Depp and Brad Pitt may get by with wearing jeans and sandals, but this could be awkward and detrimental for a professional storyboarder who wants to impress a prospective client during a meeting.

Why do I say this? I knew a guy who went to one meeting at an agency wearing sandals, and I heard the comments that were made about it afterward. Believe me, you don't want to wear sandals to a professional meeting! On the other hand, being an artist, you don't need to wear a tie, either. You are not an executive, so you are not committed to the same standard as the executives who must wear suits and ties. You want to dress neatly in appropriate clothes that are pressed and not too casual. Your clothes should be comfortable, but also show that you take your job seriously.

Your presence in the room is more important than your clothes. During the meeting, you need to be active, awake, and engaged. Turn your mobile phone off and place it on the table to show that you are accustomed to doing business without distractions and interruptions. A firm handshake and a positive attitude is what is expected of you. Also, keep in mind that your meeting is probably only one of several that might take place for the ad agency staff, so they appreciate it when you are efficient and quick so they can end the meeting.

In conclusion, here are some tips for the successful freelancer:

- In the beginning of your career you want to have your mobile phone on as much as you can (well, not during meetings, of course), so that you can be easily contacted in the event of a job offer.

- Always show up for scheduled meetings, even if you are called at the last minute. Don't be difficult.

- Avoid being irritated if the agency asks for one more revision. Instead, just see if there is a budget for the changes you have been making.

- Keep all of your work in an organized archive, preferably in chronological order, so that you can always find an old job when needed.

- Do backups and always save your work while doing it. Make copies. Do not trust your computer entirely.

- Keep track of your invoices and payments.

- Always have extra work supplies in the house (printer toner, papers, pens, etc.).

- Do not limit yourself only to storyboard jobs. Work on something else at the same time, like your art project or even a comic book, but definitely illustration work.

- Always submit work within deadline. If you are not sure that you will be able to deliver in time, call your clients to inform them and to work out a solution.

- Keep your recent projects on the desk until you have sent the invoices for it. This will help you to remember the economic side of the job.

- Be negotiable on fees and realize that sometimes you have to accept lower-paying jobs in order to always have jobs to do.

- Buy a pet! Owning a pet will force you to get away from your desk and out of the house sometimes. You need to get daily exercise, fresh air, and sunshine. You also need to make sure you get out for some fun!

My Typical Day

I am an early bird. I like to take advantage of every daylight hour to complete my work and enjoy working on my projects. I am the kind of person who is ready to get moving right from the moment that I open my eyes. Well, of course, I need my coffee to start my day properly, but I do like to start early and not waste any time in getting on with my day. I mostly work from home in my studio that I have organized in the most effective way for my needs. I don't like to become distracted by looking for tools, office supplies, papers, or reference material when I am working, so everything has a place and I try to keep everything in its place. I work from two large desks — my computer is at one of them and my tools are at the other.

Because I am up early, between 6 and 7 a.m., I can take advantage of the silence and quietness of the morning to work on my personal projects, writing or drawing before the phone starts ringing a little after 9 a.m. As the business day begins, I get calls from agencies, production companies, and/or directors with whom I frequently work. They want to schedule meetings, discuss projects, and so forth. It's not always the same every day. Calls can come from different places and countries, and jobs can come from various media. These days, I also get jobs by e-mail and, many times, I barely speak with the sender over the phone.

Sometimes the day ends up being pretty quiet. In that case, I sit in my studio and record some music or I watch movies. I keep a good archive of new releases and classic films. If I am going through a slow period with work, perhaps around holidays or festivities, I usually travel. I like to visit new places. During slow times I also surf the Internet for inspiration and to purchase reference books and movies for my infinite collection.

If I get a call for a job that is in the city, I schedule a face-to-face meeting. If the call is for a job in another country, I usually receive instructions and we discuss the project by e-mail. Occasionally, I get a call for an important job which requires me to travel for a few days. No matter where the job is, once I get the brief, I immediately review it to be sure that I know ahead of time what the job will entail and how much time it will require so I can organize my day accordingly. Remaining organized to ensure plenty of time to complete the work successfully and on deadline is important to me. I believe organization is one of my strongest skills and I encourage all beginning storyboard artists to learn the skill of organization.

As soon as I can, I produce sketches for the job and forward those to the company so I can receive feedback that will help me complete the job. In general, my sketches are self-explanatory, but sometimes further explanation or changes are needed. Even though they may be rough, the sketches are clear so the client can provide me with the comments necessary to proceed with the cleanup.

The responses to my sketches usually come in throughout the morning, which means that, most of the time, I have time for lunch like a proper human being. However, there are times when I have several jobs scheduled with tight deadlines and I must juggle a crazy schedule, and if it weren't for my girlfriend, I would simply starve because I wouldn't stop to prepare food and eat. Once I receive comments on the sketches, I continue working through to completion of the project. Completion of a project on time is my priority for each day.

When I work with feature films, I am usually obligated to attend long meetings with directors. The meetings are usually held at the directors' studios. When necessary, I travel. Otherwise, I am content to work from my studio, and I must admit that modern technologies, such as Skype, have made it very easy for us freelancers to communicate with people who are anywhere in the world. I am most comfortable when working in my studio because I can manage several tasks at the same time from there. While I'm waiting for comments to come in, I can continue to work a bit on my projects or simply do some housecleaning, bookkeeping, or research.

Along with my storyboarding work, I also run my own production company and occasionally direct music videos or short films. This keeps me busy with exciting and rewarding work, and there are also time-consuming, mundane tasks, such as going over the books with my accountant. When completing mundane tasks, I wish I could spend my time doing other things, but even the boring details are important in any business and profession.

By the time the afternoon rolls around, things usually quiet down a bit in the studio. Everyone has left the office and the phone usually stops ringing constantly, so I can settle into my most creative time of the day. Well, actually, when I am on a job things don't quiet down too much. I will continue to receive comments and revision requests and adjustments to the scripts at any time throughout the day, even late into the afternoon or into the weekend. I am quite used to it and I know how to manage my time, but I have noticed how some of my friends panic at the very idea of being in my position. I have kept the habit of considering the weekends as the same as any other day of the week. That is because I don't necessarily take weekends off work, but I may take a day or two off during the week if the schedule allows it. If there is something else I want to do on Thursday, I will take off Thursday and then work on Saturday or Sunday. Setting your schedule for your convenience is one of the advantages of being a freelancer. You can take a break in the middle of the week if you want to, and make up the working hours in the evening or on the weekend. It doesn't matter so much when you work, as long as you meet your deadlines and are available for business conversations as needed.

Some days I get more than one job per day; other days I won't get any jobs at all. On the days when I get multiple jobs, it can be quite stressful to handle all of the meetings and the work. There may be scheduling conflicts. To handle this, I have learned to utilize every minute available for working while switching back and forth between jobs. While I wait for comments on one job, I will work on another one. I can do this because, as I said before, I like to be organized and my desktop is always clean, so I can easily put away one job and set up another. It also helps tremendously that I have all of my tools and supplies at hand's reach. This is one of the key factors in working smoothly and without distraction and interruption.

Now, it might seem like I spend the whole day working, but it's not really like that. My life is not all work and no play. Even though some days are busier than others, I often have plenty of time throughout the day to take breaks and enjoy a nice walk, watch movies, play my guitar, cook meals, and so forth. When the day is over I usually have time to enjoy watching a movie or a TV series.

As I said before, every day is different. I enjoy the versatility. It's exciting to get a call from a director who needs a storyboard for a music video because that is not something I do every day, and I meet some interesting people. I have worked with some of the world's most famous directors and with international stars such as Madonna, Radiohead, Moby, Roxette, The Cardigans, Oasis, and more. Sometimes, it works out for me to meet the artist backstage. I was able to meet with Radiohead, and I have quite a collection of memorabilia and signed records. It's pretty nice also to be invited to the movie premieres of the films I worked on, and actually, it is also the best way to meet new contacts. Working in the entertainment industry is all about contacts. When I work with games, I learn months before what will hit the market, and looking at such works in progress is definitely an exciting experience.

Recently, I visited some postproduction and special-effect facilities in London. These are companies I worked with indirectly. I never deal with these types of jobs, but I am involved in the production phase with the directors, and it is really gratifying knowing that my storyboards eventually end up on the walls of the studios that produce the effects for *Narnia*, *Harry Potter*, and *Avatar*. It is very gratifying, indeed.

Being an independent artist also gives me full freedom and mobility, and I have been traveling since I left Italy for the first time. Los Angeles is becoming my second home since many of my contacts have moved there over the years, opening doors to new contacts for me. Otherwise, I am fully operative throughout all of Europe.

CONCLUSION

THE STORYBOARD ARTIST / Giuseppe Cristiano

When I decided to become a freelancer back in the 1980s, almost nobody knew what the word meant or what kind of profession I was getting into. Some of my closest acquaintances and friends were really worried about my choice, and frankly they much preferred me getting a proper job in an office, possibly with having earned a degree. There is nothing wrong with that, I suppose, but my vision was much wider than that. I was also starting to feel that my hometown had become too little and limited for me.

I finished my studies and it was time to make new decisions about choosing a university course and focusing on my future direction. However, I felt that wasn't what I wanted in life. It seemed that the only other alternative was to get a job quickly, and in the small town where I lived, the possibilities were severely limited. Given my choices, it wasn't such a hard decision for me to leave at that point and to at least take a look at what other possibilities existed out there for me.

But of course I didn't have a clue about what I wanted to achieve. All I knew was that I wanted to work with something creative, artistic, exciting. I wanted to write, draw comics, illustrate. Yes, to many people I was viewed as a dreamer. But you can never give up your dreams or you will not achieve them. Of all the advice I could offer you, this is the most important: Don't give up on your dreams!

The second most important advice that I can offer is to go ahead and try for what you want, even if you are unsure about what you are doing. Take the risk, albeit a calculated risk is best. You will never know if it's right for you if you don't try it. For example, I left my hometown and headed to Milan where I made contact with comics publishers. I had had some minor experience working with comics for small local magazines and fanzines, but I wasn't an established professional. I didn't have a clear idea of how a comics publishing house worked. Nevertheless, I managed to arrange a meeting with a couple of publishers and walked right into the room as though I knew all there was to know about the profession. I wasn't haughty and didn't give them the impression of being inexpert or anything, but I was confident in my ability to do the work. I got my first assignments.

In the beginning, I was assigned small jobs, writing little stories, mostly fillers for their magazines. But this was enough for me to prove that I was eager to work and that I had ideas. Speaking of ideas, I think the thing I did that most impressed my first publisher was that as soon as I stepped in, I started proposing ideas and new projects. It was quite naive, I believe, but courageous, and he liked my approach so he gave me a chance. I created some minor characters that he was running in one of his best-selling trendy magazines, and so I began also publishing my drawings. From there, it was a long road before I could say that I had much stability in my job, but it was certainly a good start.

One important thing I want to emphasize is that even though I had a job, I still continued to look for more jobs. This is a habit that I still have today, and is something a freelancer should always keep in mind. Never rest on your laurels. For freelancers, there will also be periods of time when there is little or no work, and if you are prepared, chances are that you will be able to move forward and upward. I have met quite a few colleagues who left freelancing and moved on to more secure jobs as the freelance lifestyle was no longer appropriate for where they were in their lives. This often happens when freelancers start a family and require more security in their finances. But I have also known many freelancers with families who were able to meet their family financial responsibilities successfully while freelancing. Freelance storyboarding can support a person or family if time is managed well and the freelancer is diligent in seeking out jobs and completing them on schedule. It is often simply a matter of self-discipline and management on the freelancer's part. If you continue to learn your craft and develop a good portfolio and reputation in the industry, and constantly make new contacts, you can have fairly steady work.

I continued freelancing in the comics industry, and had a couple of brutal experiences with storyboarding because I was not ready for it when I first stepped into it. Storyboarding was a different world altogether and the art took me by surprise. I had no knowledge of the advertising field and didn't know what was expected. Therefore, my first jobs did not meet the industry standards; they weren't good enough.

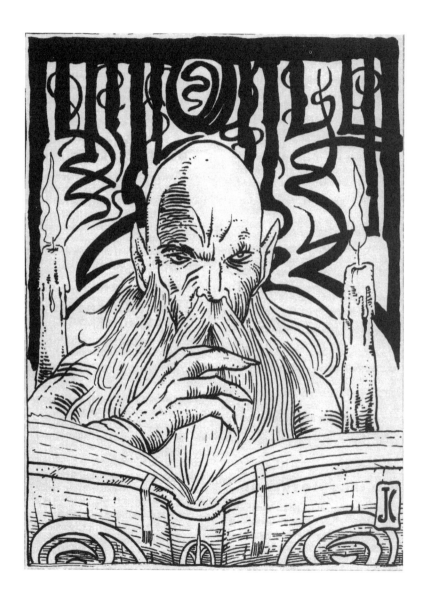

One great opportunity for me as an artist was when I had the chance to produce some work for the board game Dungeons & Dragons. I think I was replacing an artist who was no longer available for the job. I suppose it was pure luck. The job provided me with great exposure and personal satisfaction.

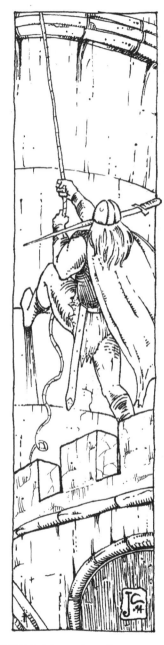

Here is another important tip: Keep learning. Be curious about things around you, especially if they relate to your work. If someone suddenly calls you from a game company, for example, to produce a few concept art illustrations, you must learn all you can about gaming. Go to your local store and see what's out there, buy some magazines, search the Net for information, read about it, learn the terms and techniques, prepare yourself for the meeting. If you are going into someone's office for a particular job, you'd better be prepared to leave a good impression. I didn't do that on my first jobs. I took the storyboard jobs as an assignment outside of my regular work, and I went completely off track with one of them. I drew a comic strip instead of the board they needed. Basically, I created for the wrong media all together.

Years later, when the occasion to work with storyboards presented itself again, I knew more about the job. This was purely by chance, as I was still not interested in pursuing storyboarding as a career. I had learned the language of film because I had a huge interest in the motion picture industry. This put me on a good track to complee the job somewhat successfully. Of course, I needed experience, and what better way to gain experience than by just trying. So I did. I kept going and looked for assignments. Then I realized that it wasn't just my hometown that felt small. I knew I needed to travel abroad. I had a vision of my life that I couldn't realize if I didn't expand and try for something bigger.

I started with what I knew best — comics. Soon enough, I realized that it wasn't the best field to be in, as there was a huge crisis going on in Europe and publishers were closing down many of their publications. I felt I had to start all over again, and I did that a few times, but I never gave up. I'll say it again — you must never give up if you want to accomplish your freelancing dream and goals. Make no excuses and continue in your work, or later on you'll feel guilt and remorse over what you did not do.

I had to go on also because I didn't really have any reason to give up. Life is hard sometimes, but you can never be sure what you will succeed in until you try it. You have to keep moving forward. I didn't know everything that I needed to know, as I was still a beginner. But that never kept me from believing that I could make it. I knew enough to keep on trying, and that is why I succeeded.

Meeting one of my favorite artists in Paris made me realize that I wasn't really fit for the comic industry at the time. The market had changed, and I could see that only after living abroad. I gained a different perspective from the one I had back home, and it finally became a reality to me that I could make my dreams come true, but I would have to change everything. To begin with, I would have to pursue a new area with my drawing. Storyboarding began to make perfect sense to me. I understood the use of storyboards in productions, from animation to music videos.

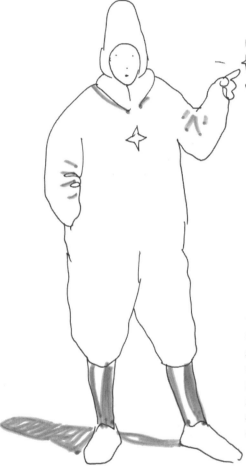

The great Moebius is always looking over my shoulder. I have framed what is probably the first most important drawing in my collection of a great artist's work, and it hangs over my desk.

Before that, I had produced work for agencies, but I never had a clear feeling for the job and didn't know what they needed the storyboard for in the first place. Also, the information I had been given was not good information. I was given just simple work-for-hire assignments in Italy by people who didn't understand the purpose of having the storyboard drawn. They were just going through the formalities. I guess I was lucky that I had a chance to try out storyboarding, but not lucky that I wasn't able to work with true professionals right from the start.

Having finally understood the importance of a good storyboard, and being inspired by the work of my idol, the artist I always wanted to imitate, Jean Giraud, aka Moebius, I started contacting advertising agencies and production companies everywhere I went. First it was France, then Sweden and all of the Scandinavian countries. Germany followed, and Spain, and England. It took a few years, but I worked hard at every job I got and created a solid reputation among my contacts. I received good recommendations and continued to network with industry professionals for more contacts and more jobs.

I started small, freelancing for various agencies, when out of the blue I got a call from a production company. It was working on an animated TV series and urgently needed a storyboard artist. I jumped on the job right away. It was a real challenge, and it gave me the chance to explore other aspects of production that I wasn't aware of. From a children's series produced by a Swedish company, I moved on to coproductions between European countries and the United States and Canada. One series was produced by Fox Family, which provided good exposure for my work.

While working with animation, I continued freelancing with the advertising and film industry. How could I find the time? I made the time because I loved what I was doing, and even though it was hard at times, it helps that I am not a person who needs many hours of sleep every night. I was also driven by the fact that I can't leave unfinished work sitting on my desk for very long. Unfinished business is something that stresses me more than having to be up all night to finish a job.

All of a sudden, I started getting calls from schools and art colleges inviting me to give storyboard lectures, first in Sweden, where I was living for the most part, and then Denmark, Norway, Spain, France, and Italy. It was at that point that I realized that there weren't any publications that focused on storyboards. I realized this because students kept asking me for reference material, manuals, and such. It seemed feasible and appropriate for me to write a manual that would be useful to students and professionals. So I did. My very first manual was published by an independent publisher that later started an online school. It was the very first storyboard school on the Internet with students from all over the world. I didn't really have much to do with the school, except for providing lectures every now and then or correcting some of the students' assignments. But I took the manual along to my meetings with prospective clients and used it as promotional material. It helped me acquire new clients.

So that leads to one more bit of advice I can leave with you: Always do things that will bring attention to your work and promote it. You can use something simple such as a portfolio, a booklet you've created, basically any samples of your work that show your talent.

After that manual, I wrote a few other books for small and big publishers, and each one of them contributed to establishing my name in the business. What has been more important through all these years has been the fact that I have always been available, 24/7, any day of the year. I never turn down a job. I always deliver within schedules, and I remain dedicated even when the job becomes tedious. I always make sure that my clients feel confident and that they can trust me, no matter what the job is.

Just recently, I had the pleasure to work with a director for a Coca Cola commercial. It was a 3D animated job, and we were meeting in a special-effects production house. On the table were a lot of amazing sketches and concept art made by the in-house artists. I asked the director why he wouldn't use any of those artists for the storyboard, and he answered that he wanted to work with me since I have storyboarded most of his previous works. He felt more comfortable with

me than any other artist. That was satisfying, knowing that someone has such trust and respect for your work. That is what a freelancer storyboard artist should look forward to.

After many years, I have finally managed to explain to my parents what I do for a living, what it is to be a freelancer. They still raise their eyebrows, but I think they pretty much get it now — and that is my biggest achievement yet, to make my parents proud of what I managed to do with my talent.

GLOSSARY

A

action match cut – Cut made between two different angles of the same action, using the subject's movement as the transition.

aerial shot – A shot that is taken from a distance overhead. It is usually taken via helicopter or plane, giving a birds-eye view.

angle – The perspective from which a camera shows the subject. The angle breaks up the monotony of a straight-on camera.

angle of view – The angle of view is the size of field of view covered by a camera lens. The angle of view is measured in degrees.

animatic – Storyboard frames which are edited together and displayed in sequence. They contain rough dialogue and a soundtrack. Animatics can be used to present ideas to advertising agencies or to test an idea for a commercial, as well as for testing the length of an animated sequence before it goes into production.

animation – The progression of story through individual drawings or CELS that are created and filmed in sequence.

aspect ratio – The relationship between the height and width of frame size. The standard, or academy's ratio, is 1:1.33. Widescreen is 1:1.85.

axis of action – Also known as the **line of action**, it is an imaginary line that separates the camera from the action before it.

B

background (BG) – Series of elements that are farthest from the camera in the visual field.

backlighting – Illumination behind an object, with the purpose of controlling the cast of shadows.

beat – A smaller dramatic unit within a scene; a scene within a scene; a change in direction of scene content.

bird's-eye view (BEV) – The view that is aerial, above an object and in the distance.

blue screen – or sometimes **green screen**. Actors are filmed against a green screen or blue screen so that the backgrounds can be changed to create the illusion that the actor has been in that location.

bridge shot – A shot used to show that there has been a time lapse or some other form of discontinuity.

brief – The process that the agency or production company uses to provide information about the treatment, script, cast choice, shooting location, direction notes, and sample pictures to the storyboard artist so the artist can develop the storyboard. The artist usually receives the information needed for the project during a briefing meeting, via e-mail or during a phone conversation.

C

camera angle – The placement of the camera in relation to the scene or subject.

canted angel shot – The method of tilting the camera to the left or to the right to give the illusion that the object within a frame is slanted.

CEL animation – Animation that uses a series of drawings on pieces of celluloid, also called CELS. An illusion of movement is created by slight changes between the drawings.

cinematography – The art of filmmaking, using cameras, film stock, and special lighting.

climax – When the story tension reaches its maximum point and opposing forces confront each other for the outcome.

close-up (CU) – A shot that shows all of the details of a larger object or shows the whole of a small object.

complementary shot – A shot that accentuates and complements another shot.

composition – The combination of light, objects, and movements that commands attention and directs the viewer in a particular direction within a frame.

continuity editing – See **screen direction**.

cover shot – See **master shot**.

crane – A large camera trolley that has a boom, where the camera is mounted on the end. The crane is designed to support multiple cameras.

crane shot – A shot that is usually an overhead view and is taken with the use of a crane.

creatives – Generally refers to those with creative jobs such as art directors and copywriters at an advertising agency.

cross dissolve – A shot transition for when one scene fades out while another fades in.

crosscutting – Cutting between two separate scenes as they unfold to show a parallel relationship between them.

cut – The transition or change from one shot to another.

cutaway – A quick shot that temporarily redirects the viewer's attention away from the main action in the film so that commentary or a change can be inserted.

D

deep focus – A photographic technique that allows all distance planes to remain in focus from close-up range to infinity.

depth of field – The distance from the camera within which objects remain in focus.

detail shot – A tighter, more highly magnified version of the **close-up** used to show a fragment of a whole subject or a small object in its total size.

distant shot – A scene photographed to give the effect of the camera being at a great distance from the action being photographed. Also called **long shot**.

dolly – A low platform that is mounted on wheels that can be steered, which supports the camera and operator.

dolly shot – When a **dolly** is used to take the shot.

dynamic composition – Pictorial composition as it changes within a moving shot.

E

editing – Creating the final draft of a film by arranging shots into scenes and sequences.

establishing shot (ES) – An opening shot of a scene. Often this is a long shot and it establishes story time and place.

exterior (EXT) – A scene that is filmed outside.

extreme close-up (ECU) – A shot that focuses on specific details of an object, such as a ring on a finger.

extreme long shot (ELS) – A shot taken at quite a distance, making the setting the focus instead of the subject.

eye-level shot – A shot taken with a camera placed at approximately the same eye-level as the film subject, instead of at the eye-level of the equipment operator. The eye-level shot places the viewer and subject on the same level.

eyeline match – A **cut** obeying the **axis of action** principle, in which the first shot shows a person looking off in one direction and the second shows a nearby space containing what he or she sees. If the person looks to the left, the following shot should imply that the looker is off-screen right.

F

fade – The **fade in** shows the gradual appearance of an image from a black or white frame, and the **fade out** shows the gradual disappearance of an image to a black or white frame. The **fade** is a transitional shot.

final cut – A film that is completely finished and will no longer be changed after the producer's or filmmaker's approval.

fish-eye lens – Lens designed to provide the maximum possible field of view.

flashback – A scene or sequence that temporarily takes the viewer backwards in time.

floor plan – A diagram of a shooting area that depicts camera positions.

fly over – See **aerial shot.**

focus pull – See **rack focus.**

follow shot – A **tracking shot, pan** or **zoom** in motion that follows a moving subject.

foreground (FG) – Elements in frame placed in the visual plane nearest the camera.

frame – A single film image. 24 frames make up one second of screen time.

full shot – A type of long shot which includes a person's body in full view, showing the head near the top of the frame and the feet near the bottom.

G

genre – A French term used to categorize groups of film that have certain commonalities in characters, plots, themes, or styles.

H

handheld shot – A shot taken with the camera operator holding the camera in his or her hand. Popular in investigative or documentary films, this is usually done to produce a wobbly effect.

headroom – Compositional space left above heads.

high angle (HA) – A shot taken from above the subject, usually from overhead.

I

insert shot – A **close-up** that shows an important detail of a scene.

intercut – An editing technique that moves between two different scenes. See also **crosscutting.**

interior (INT) – A scene that is filmed inside.

J

jump cut – A sequence of shots often used in commercials and music videos in a scene that shows real time has been interrupted by omission. Jump cuts may be used for compressing time.

juxtaposition – Creating a relationship between two objects by the placement of them in proximity or sequence.

K

kill fee – An advance payment for a contracted project whereby, in the event of the termination of a project, the fee is retained by the contractor.

L

letterboxing – An aspect ratio for television and home video that emulates **widescreen** format with black bars at the top and bottom of the screen.

lighting – The art of manipulating light and shadow in a film frame.

line of action – Also referred to as **axis of action**, the line of action is an imaginary line that separates the camera from the action before it.

long shot (LS) – A shot that shows the subject at a distance.

long take – A shot that runs for an extended duration.

loose – This term refers to the composition of a shot. Loose framing includes a great amount of space around an element.

low angle (LA) – A shot that is taken from below an object, while the camera is tilted upward. This creates the impression of looking up at the subject.

low key lighting – In order to create a gray or dark effect, the lighting is arranged to use more shadows and less illumination.

M

mainstream – A high-budget Hollywood-made film that uses well-known stars and receives massive advertising and promotion.

master shot – The viewpoint of a scene in which the relationships between subjects are clear and the entire dramatic action could be understood if no other shots were used.

match cut – A transition that cuts on common "matched" elements that connect two scenes.

matte shot – A type of special effect in which a portion of the film image is painted or created digitally and combined with live action footage in postproduction.

medium close-up (MCU) – A shot that includes the actor's upper torso and head.

medium long shot (MLS) – The subject or main object fills the entire frame. Also referred to as a **three-quarters shot**.

medium shot (MS) – Framing and shooting characters from the waist up.

mise-en-scène – The elements in frame including movement, lighting, costumes, and setting.

mockumentary – A fiction film that is a parody of the documentary style.

montage – A series of short shots that are edited together, usually without dialogue, to create a certain emotional effect or portray the passage of time.

mood board – A series of images used by an agency or production company as brainstorming material or inspiration for creating a specific mood or to define a certain style or look for a film.

motif – An image, object, spoken phrase or stylistic device that appears and reappears in a certain pattern throughout a film, gaining significance each time it appears.

moving shot – A shot in which the camera is moved as it follows a moving element.

N

narrative – The storyline of a film.

normal lens – A lens that captures what the eye would normally see.

O

180-degree rule – A filming style that dictates a camera must remain on one side of the **axis of action** while the action remains on the other. This rule helps prevent the possibility of disorienting the audience during cuts within a scene.

off camera (OC) – also referred to as **off screen** (OS). Sound that originates from outside the frame but is still identifiable as occurring within the narrative space.

omniscient point of view – A story point of view in which the narrator is omniscient or all-knowing.

open forms – Used primarily by realist film directors, these techniques are likely to be subtle and unobtrusive, with an emphasis on informal compositions and apparently haphazard designs. The frame generally is exploited to suggest a temporary masking, which arbitrarily cuts off part of the action.

over the shoulder (OTS) – A shot in which a subject who is facing us is composed using the back of the head and the shoulder of another subject in the extreme foreground as a framing device.

overlap – In sound, to carry dialogue or music from one scene to another.

P

packshot – Product shot in a commercial.

pan – A shot in which the camera rotates on its vertical axis from left to right or right to left.

parallel editing – Editing that cuts between two sequences taking place at different locations and possibly different times.

plan sequence – Scene handled in a single shot, usually a long take.

plot – A series of events that creates the storyline of a film.

point of view (POV) – The perspective from which the story is told.

point-of-view shot – A shot that shows us only what a character sees.

practical lighting – A lighting style that is realistic to what the lighting would be in real life.

production – Umbrella term encompassing both the procedure and crew involved in the actual principal photography of a film. This term can also be used to refer to the entire movie project.

progression – The traditional rising action of dramatic tension, represented by increasingly close camera angles.

property – Commonly known as **prop**, refers to any object an actor touches or uses on set during filming.

protagonist – The "good guy" or hero of a story that plays opposite the antagonist or "bad guy." The protagonist is the main character that the audience relates to and cares about.

pull back shot – A **dolly shot** or **zoom** effect that starts in **close-up** on an element and slowly widens to include more of the area surrounding the element.

R

rack focus – To shift focus from one character or element to another within a shot, such as from foreground to background. Also known as **focus pull**.

reaction shot – In a dialogue scene, the shot of a character listening while the other character is talking off camera. Most often in **close-up**.

realism – A movement in film that attempts to capture or represent reality as closely as possible.

rear projection – A technique that combines **foreground** action with a **background** that has been filmed at an earlier time. The live-action foreground is filmed in a studio, against a screen upon which the background imagery is projected from behind.

reenactments – A production that recreates an actual event as closely as possible. Often this is a historical event.

reestablishing shot – A shot that repeats an **establishing shot** near the end of a sequence.

references or reference material – Anything used by a storyboard artist to help develop a project. Reference material commonly consists of such items as graphic images, illustrations, film clips, photos, etc.

reframing – Using short **pan** or **tilt** movements of the camera to keep figures on screen or centered.

representation – How films assign meaning to what they depict, such as social groups.

retracking – Backward movement of the camera mounted on a **dolly** along a path that it has already covered in the same shot or in a previous shot within the same scene. Normally the dolly is moving on tracks.

reverse angle – A shot that is turned approximately 180 degrees in relation to a preceding shot.

rhythm – In visual composition, the pleasing repetition of images. In drama, the repetition of phrases, actions, or musical themes for increased dramatic effect.

rising action – The plot developments, including complication and rising conflict, that lead to a plot's **climax**.

rough cut – An early draft of a film that has the storyline, but has not been edited.

scene – A shot or series of shots linked by location and time.

screen direction – The right-left relationships in a scene that is set up in a master shot and determined by the position of characters and objects in frame, the direction of movement, and the characters' eye lines. **Continuity editing** attempts to keep screen direction consistent between shots. See also **axis of action**, **eyeline match**, **180-degree rule**.

sequence – A series of shots linked by time, place, and action that form a coherent unit of narrative with a specific start, middle, and end.

setting – The time and place in which a film's action occurs.

setup – Choosing a certain **camera angle**, shot size, and staging. It is normally described by the number of players in a shot. A **two-shot**, **over-the-shoulder shot**, and **close-up** are all typical setups.

shallow focus – A shot wherein a small frame area is in focus while the rest of it is blurry.

shooting board – A storyboard produced for the director and production team as a guideline during filming.

shooting script – The final script from which the film is shot.

shot – A single uninterrupted run of the camera.

single – Shot with only one subject in the frame.

slow motion – The effect of slowed action created by exposing frames in the camera at greater-than-normal speed and then projecting that footage at the normal speed of twenty-four frames per second.

special effects (F/X) – A general term for various photographic and digital manipulations in the film, such as **superimposition**, **matte shots**, and **rear projection**.

split screen – Two or more scenes on screen at the same time.

static camera – Any shot in which the camera is still, not in motion.

Steadicam™ – The invention of cameraman Garret Brown (developed in conjunction with Cinema Products, Inc.), this is a system which permits handheld filming with an image steadiness comparable to **tracking shots**. An armor redistributes the weight of the camera to the hips of the camera operator; a spring-loaded arm minimizes the motion the camera; a video monitor frees the camera operator from the eyepiece.

storyboard – Series of drawings that suggest how a scene or film might look once filmed.

style – A director's personal way of treating material, including staging of camera and performers, script elements, and music.

subjective camera – Technique that presents the viewpoint of a character in a scene. See also **point of view**.

subjective point of view – A point of view that is limited; the narrator is unaware of some things occurring in the narrative.

superimposition – The exposure of more than one image on the same filmstrip.

swish pan – A panning shot in which the intervening scene moves past too quickly to be observed. It approximates psychologically the action of the human eye as it moves from one subject to another. Also called **whip pan** or **zip pan**.

T

take – One continuous recording of a shot.

talking heads – Medium shots of people talking, with minimal action occurring in the shot.

telephoto lens – A lens that can act like a telescope. Often used in sports, news, and documentary.

testimony – Statements made by people witnessing an event or going through an experience themselves.

theme – A dominant idea made concrete through its representation by the characters, action, and imagery of the film.

three-quarters shot – A shot that shows a character from the knees up.

three shot – A medium shot that contains three people.

tight framing – Usually in close shots. The mise-en-scène is so carefully balanced and harmonized that the subject photographed has little or no freedom of movement.

tilt – The upward and downward movement of the camera.

timing – The control of objective and subjective time.

tracking shot – A shot that is taken while the camera moves on a wheeled platform.

traveling shot – Any shot that requires the camera to move from one location to another. **crane shot** and **tracking shot** are both traveling shots. A **pan shot** is not a traveling shot since the camera stays in one location.

treatment – An outline of a film script which describes the general story without the use of dialogue.

two shot – A medium shot with two people in it.

U

underlighting – Illumination from a point below the figures in the scene.

V

visualization – The mental visual image of an event in a single shot. Also known as **conceptualization**.

W

whip pan – see **swish pan**.

wide angle lens – A type of lens that exaggerates the disparity between the foreground and background within a film frame. Objects in the foreground become disproportionately larger, while those in the background become disproportionately smaller.

widescreen – Any image with an aspect ratio greater than the Academy standard of 1.33:1. The most common widescreen aspect ratio is 1.85:1

wipe – A visual effect in which one image replaces another by seemingly pushing it off the screen.

Z

zip pan – see **swish pan**.

zoom – An optical effect that increases or decreases the magnification of an object in frame, making it appear larger or smaller than it really is. The effect is achieved through changing the focal length of a lens.

ABOUT THE AUTHOR

Giuseppe Cristiano is a professional storyboard artist and creative jack-of-all-trades who works with the heavy hitters of the international advertising, interactive entertainment, and film industries.

Originally from Italy, he started out as a comic artist, where he honed his drawing skills before branching out to become an illustrator and storyboard artist for advertising agencies and film production companies throughout Europe and the United States. He regularly freelances for companies such as Saatchi & Saatchi, Ogilvy, DDB, BBDO Worldwide, Ridley Scott Associates, Fox Family, A&E, HBO, BBC, Warner Bros., and many others.

In addition to his bread-and-butter work as a storyboard artist, he is a much sought-after illustrator, producing concept art for films and animation, illustrations for magazines, books, and comics.

He has also written and directed a number of shorts, music videos, and animation. When time permits, he gives classes and seminars on storyboarding for cinema and television, and scriptwriting and comic illustration at colleges, film schools, and art institutes in Europe. He is currently working with students from Padua on an online teaching project aimed at adapting modern technology for use in the classroom.

In his spare time, Giuseppe produces and records music under his artist name J Crist. He plays several instruments and collects guitars.

His website is: www.giuseppecristiano.com.

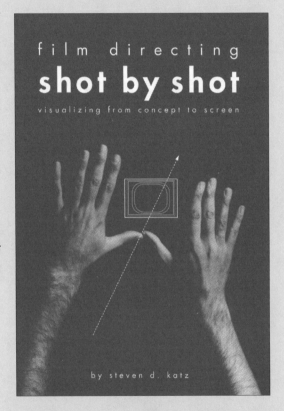

FROM WORD TO IMAGE - 2ND ED.
STORYBOARDING AND THE FILMMAKING PROCESS

MARCIE BEGLEITER

BEST SELLER

"We are telling thousands of stories through media that did not even exist eight short years ago. On the home front, entry level HD camcorders mean that even beginning students have access to low-cost professional-quality image-making. GarageBand offers music studio features to score your project and YouTube affords access to a world-wide audience. Never have so many visual storytellers been able to say so much with so little to so many."

> — from the Introduction
> *From Word to Image*

This classic text on storyboarding and visual communication has been updated with information on new media and expanded to incorporate an in-depth study of the use of color in storytelling.

"*Begleiter has given the subject its own place in the sun through this groundbreaking practical guide and historic companion.*"

> — *Directors Guild of America* magazine

"*Begleiter's book is very thorough; 18 years of experience in the motion-picture industry have given her the tools to illustrate complex concepts with great visual immediacy.*"

> — *American Cinematographer*

"*From Word to Image is wonderful not only as an examination of the how-to's of storyboard art, but is full of rich film history. It demystifies an aspect of filmmaking that benefits everyone involved; from directors, to cinematographers, to production designers.*"

> — Joe Petricca, dean, AFI Conservatory

MARCIE BEGLEITER is an author, educator, and designer specializing in visualization and interdisciplinary design solutions. She founded Filmboards, a visualization agency whose client list includes Paramount, Tristar, New Line, and ABC. In academia, she was Founding Director of the Integrated Learning Program, a multi-disciplinary design curriculum at Otis College of Art and Design. She has also served on the faculties of the International Film School in Cologne, Germany, the American Film Institute, and Art Center College of Design. Ms. Begleiter is also a playwright and a member of the Actor's Studio Playwright/Directors unit.

MARCIE BEGLEITER

from word to image

Storyboarding and the Filmmaking Process
2ND ED

$26.95 | 248 PAGES | ORDER NUMBER 136RLS | ISBN: 9781932907674

MASTER SHOTS VOL 2
100 WAYS TO SHOOT GREAT DIALOGUE SCENES

CHRISTOPHER KENWORTHY

Building on the success of the best-selling *Master Shots*, this book goes much deeper, revealing the great directors' secrets for making the most of the visual during the usual static dialogue scene. A strong scene is determined from where you put the camera and how you position and direct your actors. This is especially true when shooting dialogue. The techniques in *Master Shots, Vol. 2* ensure that every plot point, every emotion, and every subtle meaning is communicated clearly.

This is the first book to show how important it is to shoot dialogue well. What's the point of opening your scene with a great camera move, if you then just shoot the actors like a couple of talking heads? *Master Shots, Vol. 2* gives you control of dialogue scenes, whether you're shooting two characters or a room filled with multiple conversations.

Using examples from well-known films, the book gives 100 techniques, lavishly illustrated with movie frame-grabs, and overhead diagrams, to show exactly what you need to get the required result. At all times, the techniques have been broken down to their core points, so they will work on a fully equipped Hollywood set, or with the most basic video camera.

"*A terrific sequel to the first* Master Shots. *If there's a cool way to move the camera, Kenworthy has explained it to us. I can't wait to get this book into my students' hands.*"

– John Badham, director, *Saturday Night Fever*, *WarGames*; author, *I'll Be in My Trailer*

"Master Shots, Vol 2 *will inspire every filmmaker to think carefully about placement and movement of actors as seen through the camera lens. This book increases the reader's appreciation for the critical work of the cinematographer and the director as they speak the language of film through images.*"

– Mary J. Schirmer, screenwriter, screenwriting instructor, *www.screenplayers.net*

CHRISTOPHER KENWORTHY has worked as a writer, director, and producer for the past ten years. He directed the feature film *The Sculptor*, which played to sold-out screenings in Australia and received strong reviews. Recent works include sketch comedy for the BBC's *Scallywagga*, a title sequence for National Geographic Channel, visual effects for 3D World, music videos for Pieces of Eight Records and Elefant Records, and an animated wall projection for The Blue Room Theatre in Perth, Australia. Kenworthy is the author of the best-selling *Master Shots*, two novels: *The Winter Inside* and *The Quality of Light*, and many short stories. Current projects include screenwriting, several directing assignments, and the development of additional *Master Shots* applications.

$26.95 | 240 PAGES | ORDER NUMBER 167RLS | ISBN: 9781615930555

24 HOURS | 1.800.833.5738 | WWW.MWP.COM

MASTER SHOTS VOL 1 - 2ND ED.
100 ADVANCED CAMERA TECHNIQUES TO GET AN EXPENSIVE LOOK ON YOUR LOW-BUDGET MOVIE

CHRISTOPHER KENWORTHY

BEST SELLER

Master Shots gives filmmakers the techniques they need to execute complex, original shots on any budget. By using powerful master shots and well-executed moves, directors can develop a strong style and stand out from the crowd. Most low-budget movies look low-budget, because the director is forced to compromise at the last minute. *Master Shots* gives you so many powerful techniques that you'll be able to respond, even under pressure, and create knockout shots. Even when the clock is ticking and the light is fading, the techniques in this book can rescue your film, and make every shot look like it cost a fortune.

Each technique is illustrated with samples from great feature films and computer-generated diagrams for absolute clarity.

"The camera is just a tool, and anyone who thinks making a movie is about knowing how to use a camera is destined to fail. In Master Shots, *Christopher Kenworthy* offers an excellent manual for using this tool to create images that arouse emotional impact and draw the viewer into the story. No matter what camera you're using, don't even think about turning it on until you've read this book!"

— Catherine Clinch, publisher
MomsDigitalWorld.com

"Though one needs to choose any addition to a film book library carefully, what with the current plethora of volumes on cinema, Master Shots *is an essential addition to any worthwhile collection.*"

— Scott Essman, publisher,
Directed By magazine

CHRISTOPHER KENWORTHY has worked as a writer, director, and producer for the past ten years. He directed the feature film *The Sculptor*, which played to sold-out screenings in Australia and received strong reviews. Recent works include sketch comedy for the BBC's *Scallywagga*, a title sequence for National Geographic Channel, visual effects for 3D World, music videos for Pieces of Eight Records and Elefant Records, and an animated wall projection for The Blue Room Theatre in Perth, Australia. Kenworthy is the author of the best-selling *Master Shots*, two novels: *The Winter Inside* and *The Quality of Light*, and many short stories. Current projects include screenwriting, several directing assignments, and the development of additional *Master Shots* applications.

CINEMATIC STORYTELLING
THE 100 MOST POWERFUL FILM CONVENTIONS EVERY FILMMAKER MUST KNOW

JENNIFER VAN SIJL

BEST SELLER

How do directors use screen direction to suggest conflict? How do screenwriters exploit film space to show change? How does editing style determine emotional response?

Many first-time writers and directors do not ask these questions. They forego the huge creative resource of the film medium, defaulting to dialog to tell their screen story. Yet most movies are carried by sound and picture. The industry's most successful writers and directors have mastered the cinematic conventions specific to the medium. They have harnessed non-dialog techniques to create some of the most cinematic moments in movie history.

This book is intended to help writers and directors more fully exploit the medium's inherent storytelling devices. It contains 100 non-dialog techniques that have been used by the industry's top writers and directors. From *Metropolis* and *Citizen Kane* to *Dead Man* and *Kill Bill*, the book illustrates — through 500 frame grabs and 75 script excerpts — how the inherent storytelling devices specific to film were exploited.

You will learn:
· How non-dialog film techniques can advance story.

· How master screenwriters exploit cinematic conventions to create powerful scenarios.

"Cinematic Storytelling *scores a direct hit in terms of concise information and perfectly chosen visuals, and it also searches out... and finds... an emotional core that many books of this nature either miss or are afraid of.*"

— Kirsten Sheridan, director, *Disco Pigs*; co-writer, *In America*

"*Here is a uniquely fresh, accessible, and truly original contribution to the field. Jennifer van Sijll takes her readers in a wholly new direction, integrating aspects of screenwriting with all the film crafts in a way I've never before seen. It is essential reading not only for screenwriters but also for filmmakers of every stripe.*"

— Prof. Richard Walter, UCLA screenwriting chairman

JENNIFER VAN SIJLL has taught film production, film history, and screenwriting. She is currently on the faculty at San Francisco State's Department of Cinema.

$24.95 | 230 PAGES | ORDER NUMBER 35RLS | ISBN: 9781932907056

ANIMATION UNLEASHED
100 PRINCIPLES EVERY ANIMATOR, COMIC BOOK WRITER, FILMMAKER, VIDEO ARTIST, AND GAMER SHOULD KNOW

ELLEN BESEN WITH ILLUSTRATIONS BY **BRYCE HALLETT**

Animation's potential as a powerful tool for communication is just beginning to be understood. This book reveals key principles, useful for both professionals and beginners, which will help you harness the full power of this exciting and ever expanding medium.

Through close reading of key animated productions, this book uncovers and examines foundational principles for creating animation which really communicate. Key information for every facet of animation production and every application of animation whether TV series, feature film, independent filmmaking, web animation, or computer game is offered in an easy to understand format, which makes this book both a textbook and quick reference guide.

"Animation books often rely on simple formulas that illustrate mechanical approaches to solving specific problems or provide isolated answers and methods that lack further application. From years of filmmaking experience, Ellen has managed to distill conceptual principles that, once integrated, can build and enhance the tool kit a filmmaker uses to analyze and solve conceptual problems. Used properly, these thinking tools can lead the filmmaker to fresh and creative solutions to the challenges of communicating and entertaining with animation. Ellen's book is a concise window into her lifetime of experience and passion for the animation medium."

— Charlie Bonifacio, animator, *Mulan*, *Hunchback of Notre Dame*

"This book challenges the reader to think critically about what to animate, how to do it — and why. It may even unleash the unbridled animation passion that lurks deep within the psyche of every meek and unassuming animation student."

— Janet Perlman, animation director/ writer, Hulascope Studio

ELLEN BESEN is a former faculty member of Sheridan College's School of Animation and has been working in the field for over 35 years. Her career includes directing award-winning films for the National Film Board of Canada, broadcast work on the topic of animation for CBC Radio, and film curating for such organizations as the Art Gallery of Ontario. She is currently creative director of The Kalamazoo Animation Festival International and continues to teach the principles of animation filmmaking on an intensive one-on-one basis.

BRYCE HALLETT is an award-winning independent animator/cartoonist. His cartoons have been seen in TV shows such as *The Red Green Show* (CBC/PBS), *History Bites* (History Television/Comedy Network), advertisements and music videos.

CINEMATOGRAPHY FOR DIRECTORS
A GUIDE FOR CREATIVE COLLABORATION

JACQUELINE B. FROST

The essential handbook for directors and aspiring filmmakers who want to get the best visuals for their films while establishing a collaborative relationship with their cinematographer.

Through balancing interviews with working ASC cinematographers and the technical, aesthetic, and historical side of cinematography, this book guides directors toward a more powerful collaboration with their closest ally, the cinematographer. Topics include selecting a cinematographer, discussing the script with the cinematographer, choosing the appropriate visual style for the film, color palette, various film and HD formats, and postproduction processes including the digital intermediate.

"I urge all aspiring filmmakers to read Cinematography for Directors. *Frost has the ability to put the director at ease by bringing clarity to the notoriously elusive relationship between the filmmaker and the cinematographer... The numerous thrilling interviews she conducts create an empowering message: that the dynamic between the director and their cinematographer can be a relationship of understanding, ease, humor, passion and, above all, true collaboration."*

— Bryce Dallas Howard, actress (*Terminator Salvation*, *Spider-Man 3*, *As You Like It*, *Lady in the Water*, *The Village*), writer, producer, director

"Far too few books about the filmmaking process address the complex, challenging, and intensely collaborative relationship that exists between the director and the cinematographer. Drawing on her vast experience as a working cinematographer and as a film school professor, Frost deftly combines her clear appreciation of the profession of cinematography with a pragmatic guide for how to accomplish these often startling and culturally-significant moments of visual artistry."

— Denise Mann, head, UCLA Producers Program; associate professor, Department of Film, TV, Digital Media, University of California, Los Angeles

JACQUELINE B. FROST has been teaching film and video production and film history for twenty years at various universities including Miami, Penn State University, and the University of Oklahoma. She currently teaches cinematography and advanced film production at California State University, Fullerton where she is an Associate Professor. She regularly teaches a course through the UCLA extension entitled, Cinematography for Directors, on which the book is based. In addition to teaching, Jacqueline has been the cinematographer on numerous sort films, independent feature films, and documentaries that have been screened in film festivals.

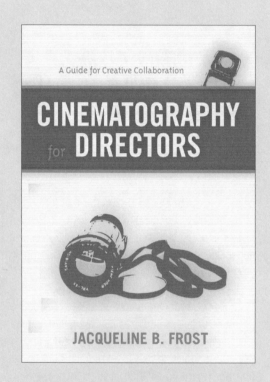

$29.95 | 292 PAGES | ORDER NUMBER 127RLS | ISBN: 9781932907551

THE MYTH OF MWP

In a dark time, a light bringer came along, leading the curious and the frustrated to clarity and empowerment. It took the well-guarded secrets out of the hands of the few and made them available to all. It spread a spirit of openness and creative freedom, and built a storehouse of knowledge dedicated to the betterment of the arts.

The essence of the Michael Wiese Productions (MWP) is empowering people who have the burning desire to express themselves creatively. We help them realize their dreams by putting the tools in their hands. We demystify the sometimes secretive worlds of screenwriting, directing, acting, producing, film financing, and other media crafts.

By doing so, we hope to bring forth a realization of 'conscious media' which we define as being positively charged, emphasizing hope and affirming positive values like trust, cooperation, self-empowerment, freedom, and love. Grounded in the deep roots of myth, it aims to be healing both for those who make the art and those who encounter it. It hopes to be transformative for people, opening doors to new possibilities and pulling back veils to reveal hidden worlds.

MWP has built a storehouse of knowledge unequaled in the world, for no other publisher has so many titles on the media arts. Please visit www.mwp.com where you will find many free resources and a 25% discount on our books. Sign up and become part of the wider creative community!

Onward and upward,

Michael Wiese
Publisher/Filmmaker